Modern Judgements

FREUD

MODERN JUDGEMENTS

Freud

MODERN JUDGEMENTS

edited by

FRANK CIOFFI

MACMILLAN

First published 1973 by
THE MACMILLAN PRESS LTD
London and Basingstoke
Associated companies in New York Dublin
Melbourne Johannesburg and Madras

SBN 333 01016 7

Printed in Great Britain by
HAZELL WATSON AND VINEY LTD
Aylesbury, Bucks

Contents

Chronology

1856   Sigmund Freud born in Freiburg, Moravia.
1873   Begins medical studies at Vienna University.
1885–6 Scholarship permits visit to Charcot's clinic in Paris.
1887   Start of friendship and correspondence with Wilhelm Fliess. Begins the use of hypnotic suggestion.
1889   Visits Bernheim, Charcot's chief rival, at Nancy to study therapeutic hypnosis.
1893   Publishes with Breuer a paper, 'On the Psychical Mechanism of Hysteria'.
1895   Embraces seduction theory. Publication, jointly with Breuer, of *Studies on Hysteria*.
1896   Publishes three papers on the aetiology of nervous conditions indicting infantile sexual seduction in hysteria, masturbation in neuraesthenia, and frustrated sexual excitation and abstinence in anxiety.
1897   Self-analysis and the private abandonment of the seduction theory and recognition of infantile sexuality and the Oedipus complex.
1900   Publication of *The Interpretation of Dreams*.
1904   Publication in book form of *The Psychopathology of Everyday Life*, which further extended his theories to normal psychology.
1905   Publications of *Three Essays on the Theory of Sexuality*, containing the theory of the polymorphous perversity of infancy and the regressive character of homosexuality. Publication of the case of 'Dora' featuring the first extended use of dream interpretation for diagnostic purposes.
1906   Publicly renounces the seduction theory. Jung becomes a supporter.

1909   Invited to the United States to lecture at Clark University. Case history of first child analysis (Little Hans) produced as confirmation of theories of infantile sexuality, the Oedipus complex and castration anxiety.

1911   Split with Adler. Publishes theory of paranoia in the form of an analysis of the autobiography of Dr Schreber.

1913–14   *Totem and Taboo:* arguing for the origin of morality and religion in a primal parricide.

1914   Secession of Jung. Publishes 'On the History of the Psycho-Analytic Movement'; introduces the notion of narcissm.

1915–17   Publication of *Introductory Lectures,* originally delivered at the University of Vienna.

1918   Publishes last major case history, 'The Wolf Man', (written by 1915).

1920   Publication of *Beyond the Pleasure Principle,* introducing the concepts of the 'repetition compulsion' and the 'death instinct'.

1921   Publication of *Group Psychology and the Analysis of the Ego.*

1923   Publication of *The Ego and The Id,* a revised account of the mind. Beginning of cancer.

1926   Publication of *Inhibitions, Symptoms, and Anxiety* (*The Problem of Anxiety*).

1930   Publication of *Civilisation and its Discontents.* Award of Goethe Prize.

1933   Publication of *New Introductory Lectures,* incorporating theoretical innovations of the past two decades.

1936   Eightieth birthday celebrations. Election as Corresponding Member of the Royal Society.

1938   German invasion of Austria. Leaves Vienna for London. Works on *An Outline of Psycho-Analysis,* the final, definitive but unfinished exposition of psychoanalysis. Publishes *Moses and Monotheism* on which he was engaged from 1934.

1939   Dies in London on 23 September.

Introduction

WHEN did Freud arrive? What was the situation on which he impinged? What sort of reception did he receive and how it is to be accounted for? There is a received answer to these questions: that due to their painful truth Freud's views only slowly became known and then only to be reviled in a manner almost unprecedented.

In his life of Freud, Ernest Jones tells us that 'in the first years of the century Freud and his writings were either quietly ignored or else they would be mentioned with a sentence or two of disdain as if not deserving any serious attention'.[1] Abraham Brill also paints a picture of Freud 'surrounded by a sceptical and hostile world . . . his theories of the neuroses . . . rejected and derided by the neurologists and psychiatrists of his time'.[2]

These remarks are more misleading than the necessity of representing a complex situation in a mnemonic formula can justify. Not only because of the fact, documented by Bry and Rifkin and endorsed by Henri Ellenberger in his monumental *The Discovery of the Unconscious*, that 'for the time during which Freud was supposed to have been ignored' he received 'a great many signs of recognition and extraordinary respect', but for another reason.[3] In the passages I quoted, Jones speaks broadly of 'Freud and his writings', and Brill refers quite as broadly to 'the theories of the neuroses which (Freud) formulated during this period'. We all think we know to which writings and to which theories these remarks refer but like most accounts of Freud's reception during the decade or so after *Studies on Hysteria*, they mislead by their failure

1. Ernest Jones, *Sigmund Freud: Life and Work*, vol. 2 (London, 1958) p. 123.

2. A. Brill, *Lectures on Psychoanalytic Psychiatry* (London, 1948) p. 7.

3. Ilse Bry and Alfred H. Rifkin, 'Freud and the History of Ideas: Primary Sources, 1886–1900', *Science and Psychoanalysis*, vol. 5 (New York, 1962) p. 28; Henri Ellenberger, *The Discovery of the Unconscious* (New York, 1970) particularly pp. 450, 454–5, 480.

to take note of a rather surprising fact, to appreciate the significance of which a certain amount of background is needed. Sometime between 1893 and 1895 Freud came to believe that a sexual seduction in early childhood was an indispensable precondition for the development of psycho-neurotic illness. He proclaimed this conclusion in three papers published in 1896, one of which was also delivered as a lecture to his Vienna colleagues.

Freud was confirmed in this conviction by one of his own dreams, which he interpreted as evidence of an unconscious wish to have sexual relations with his nine year old daughter. But some time later an infantile reminiscence of having been excited by the sight of his mother naked suggested an alternative explanation of the appearance of seduction material in his patients' productions: that they were distorted reminiscences of the children's erotic impulses towards the cross-sexed parent. In any case, for whatever reason, by September 1897 Freud had changed his mind and decided that the seduction theory was mistaken.

The startling fact referred to above is that Freud did not *publicly* repudiate the infantile seduction theory of hysteria until eight years later. Its bearing on the question of Freud's reception is that it is difficult to say at this date how much of the incredulity and derision Freud encountered in those years was provoked by claims which he himself had already privately rejected and which form no part of what came to be known as psychoanalysis. As late as 1909, Emile Kraeplin, in the eighth edition of his textbook, was still under the impression that Freud adhered to the seduction theory.[4]

We have seen how misleading is the view that the usual response to the views that we today associate with Freud was silence or derision. It is more difficult to decide whether his celebrity was so long delayed

4. This fact doesn't seem to have been taken in properly by students of the psycho-analytic movement. Marjorie Brierly, Marthe Robert, Erik Ericson, J. A. C. Brown and J. C. Burnham all appear to confound, at least intermittently, the date at which Freud publicly renounced the seduction theory with the date at which he privately abandoned it. Other writers seem to forget that he ever held it. For example, David Stafford-Clark, in his book *What Freud Really Said* (London, 1967), cites as evidence of the unreasoning incredulity and hostility with which Freud's views were met, the criticism he received on the occasion on which he addressed the Society of Neurologists and Psychiatrists in 1896 with Krafft-Ebing in the chair. This was the meeting at which Freud expounded the infantile seduction theory, which he himself later described as having collapsed 'under the weight of its own improbability'.

that an explanation is called for. Our problem is threefold. When do we start counting? When do we stop? And how long is long?

Writing in 1932, Franz Alexander said of Freud's theories: 'All these concepts are today not only generally accepted, but they have already become emotionally assimilated, and like the theory of evolution or the cosmological doctrine of the planetary systems are now an integral part of modern thinking. . . .'[5] When did this state of affairs come about?

In his useful book on Freud's precursors, Lancelot Law Whyte refers to 'the years after the First World War when psychoanalysis was a novelty', thus envincing a common misconception. It is true that the character in Scott Fitzgerald's *This Side of Paradise* (1920), who describes herself as 'hipped on Freud and all that' is an advanced female, and that as late as 1918 H. L. Mencken could write: 'hard upon the heels of . . . the Montessori method, vers libre and the music of Stravinsky, psychoanalysis now comes to intrigue and harass the sedentary multipara who seek refuge in the women's clubs from the horrible joys of home life.'[6]

But Alfred Kuttner, who helped Brill with his translation of *The Interpretation of Dreams* and did much to publicise psychoanalysis among American intellectuals, remarked in 1922 in his contribution to the book *Civilization in the United States* that 'Freud after an initial resistance rapidly became epidemic in America'. In her contribution to the same volume the sexual reformer, Elsie Clews Parsons, refers to the age as 'this post-Freudian day'.[7] A year later D. H. Lawrence referred to the Oedipus complex as 'a household word . . . a commonplace of tea table chat'.

An allusion in Clifford Allen's *Modern Discoveries in Medical Psychology* (London, 1937) to a period around 1914 when 'society ladies became interested in psychoanalysis and went about talking of their complexes', provoked Ernest Jones to object that

> we have several times come across vague allusions to this supposed craze of society women for psychoanalysis, but we have never seen it placed in time so precisely. Unfortunately the author does not locate it in space so

5. F. Alexander, 'Psychoanalysis and Medicine', *Mental Hygiene*, XVI, (January 1932) pp. 63–84.

6. H. L. Mencken, 'Rattling the Subconscious', *The Smart Set* (September 1918) p. 138.

7. Harold E. Stearns (ed.), *Civilization in the United States* (New York, 1922) p. 311.

definitely as in time. Viennese society had certainly other things with which to occupy itself in 1914, at the beginning of the war, and London had hardly heard of the subject at that time.[8]

But it is to New York that Dr Allen's remark, though no doubt hyperbolic, has some application. By 1916 there were some five hundred self-styled psychoanalysts practising there. And it was there that Mabel Dodge Luhan conducted a salon at which psychoanalysis was a favourite topic of discussion and which Freud's American translator, the analyst Abraham Brill, was invited to address.

Mrs Luhan, who was analysed by both Brill and Smith Ely Jelliffe, though no mere society lady, did go about talking of her complexes:

> I enjoyed my visits . . . it became an absorbing game to play with oneself, reading one's motives, and trying to understand the symbols by which the soul expressed itself . . . I longed to draw others into the new world where I found myself: a world where things fitted into a set of definitions and terms that had never even been dreamt of. It simplified all problems to name them. There was the Electra complex, and the Oedipus complex and there was the libido with its manifold activities. . . .[9]

Among those who argue that Freud's celebrity was unduly belated are Shakow and Rapaport, but they overlook the fact that Freud's works were written in a foreign language which, though it may have been known to a number of doctors and psychologists, had to be translated before they were accessible to the educated public.[10] The *Three Essays on Sexuality* was translated in 1910 as were the lectures which Freud delivered at Clark University. What is generally considered his greatest work, *The Interpretation of Dreams*, was not translated into English until 1913, and he was completely untranslated until Brill produced a selection of his papers on the psycho-neuroses in 1909.

Though in the absence of agreed criteria the reader must decide for himself just how long long is, these facts do much to mitigate the impression of belated celebrity that may be produced by thinking of Freud's claims on the attention of the English-speaking world as dating from the turn of the century.

Perhaps the most useful observation to make with respect to the

8. *International Journal of Psychoanalysis*, XVIII (1937) pp. 483–4.

9. Mabel Dodge Luhan, *Makers and Shakers* (New York, 1936) pp. 439–40.

10. D. Shakow and D. Rapaport, *The Influence of Freud on American Psychology* (Cleveland, Ohio, 1964).

cultural climate in which Freud's early works appeared is the felt
continuity of his explanatory modes and intuitions with literary culture and folk wisdom, with what Dr Johnson referred to 'as remarks
on life, or axioms of morality as float in conversation and are trans-
mitted to the world in proverbial sentences', rather than with esoteric
scientific or philosophical speculation.

The reviewer of *Studies on Hysteria* for the *Neue Freie Presse* observed of the Breuer–Freud theory of hysteria that it was 'nothing
but the kind of psychology used by poets' – and by the rest of us he
might have added. The following stanza from one of the songs in
Tennyson's *The Princess* was often cited, both before and after Freud,
as illustrating what the *Studies on Hysteria* (1895) referred to as 'strangu-
lated affect':

> Home they brought her warrior dead
> She nor swooned nor uttered cry;
> All her maidens, watching, said,
> She must weep or she will die.[11]

Malcolm's injunction to Macduff ('Give sorrow words; the grief
that does not speak/Whispers the o'er-fraught heart and bids it break'),
or the incident in *Persuasion* when Captain Wentworth, encountering
Anne Elliot after Louisa Musgrove's accident at Lyme Regis, comments,
'I am afraid you must have suffered from the shock, and the more
from its not overpowering you at the time', might just as appositely
have been invoked.

What also tends to be insufficiently stressed in the standard accounts
of the intellectual climate in which Freud's work appeared is the cur-
rency of his sexual themes, particularly with reference to the neuroses,
but even in their more general bearings.

The reviewer of *The Studies on Hysteria* for *Brain* remarked, on its
publication in 1895: 'It is interesting to note a return, in part at least,
to the old theory of the origin of hysteria in sexual disorders.' However,
the implication that Freud was reviving a view which was moribund
would seem to be unwarranted. If we consult the entry on hysteria
in Hack Tuke's dictionary of medical psychology, published in 1892,
we find it stated that:

11. This poem was sufficiently familiar that another of its lines, the one recording the
abreaction, 'Like summer tempests came her tears', could, with a change of gender, be
used as the title of the penultimate chapter of *The Wind in the Willows*.

Among the activities artificially repressed in girls, it must be recognized that the sexual play an important part and, indeed, the frequent evidence given of dammed up sexual emotions ... have led many to regard unsatisfied sexual desire as one of the leading causes of hysteria ... forced abstinence from the gratification of any of the inherent and primitive desires must have untoward results.[12]

The view that it was the function of hysterical attacks to provoke rape was advanced in 1890 by an American physician, A. F. A. King:

... In prudish women of strong moral principle whose volition has disposed them to resist every sort of liberty or approach from the other sex [there occurs] a transient abdication of the general, volitional, and self-preservational ego, while the reins of government are temporarily assigned to the usurping power of the reproductive ego, so that the reproductive government overrules the government by volition and thus forcibly compels the woman's organism ... to allow, invite, and secure the approach of the other sex, whether she will or not, to the end that nature's imperious demands for reproduction shall be obeyed.

Dr King then proceeds to the following idyllic account of the likely sequence of events in a community uncorrupted by civilization:

Let us picture ourselves a young aboriginal Venus in one of her earliest hysteria paroxysms .... Let this Venus now be discovered by a youthful Apollo of the woods, a man with fully developed animal instincts but without moral, legal or religious restraint. ... He cannot but observe to himself: this woman is not dead; she does not look ill; she is well nourished, plump and rosy. He speaks to her; she neither hears, apparently, nor responds. Her eyes are closed. He touches, moves and handles her at his pleasure; she makes no resistance. What will this primitive Apollo do next? .... The course of nature having been followed, the natural purpose of the hysteric paroxysm being accomplished, there would remain as a result of the treatment – instead of one pining, discontented woman – two happy people and the probable beginning of a third.[13]

But this alertness to the less blatant manifestations of sexuality in human life was not confined to medical contexts.

At the beginning of the Victorian era, a diarist recorded his convic-

12. H. B. Donkin, 'Hysteria', A Dictionary of Psychological Medicine, vol. 1 (London, 1892) p. 620.
13. A. F. A. King, 'Hysteria', American Journal of Obstetrics, XXIV (1891) pp. 513–32. If Ueber Hysterie (Berlin, 1892) by 'King' is a translation of this, then it was in Freud's library.

tion that a young woman's dismay at the prospect of ending her pla-
tonic association with an older man 'was sexual though she did not
know it'. (It enhances the piquancy of this observation that the young
woman concerned was Queen Victoria; the man was Lord Melbourne
and the diarist Greville.) And consider the following reflections on the
relations between sexuality and the appreciation of beauty:

> ... Some of the most conspicuous elements of beauty ought to be called
> sexual ... because they owe their fascination in a great measure to the parti-
> cipation of our sexual life in the reactions which they cause. Sex is not the
> only object of sexual passion. When love lacks its specific object, when it
> does not yet understand itself, or has been sacrificed to some other interest,
> we see the stifled fire bursting out in various directions. One is religious
> devotion, another is zealous philanthropy, a third is the fondling of pet
> animals, but not the least fortunate is the love of nature, and of art .... [14]

We would confidently have cited these remarks as a striking example of Freud's influence in facilitating the tendency to see the operation of sexuality in areas previously considered remote from it if we
did not know that it is what Santayana was telling his classes at Harvard
in the early nineties.

I shall follow Shakow and Rapaport in dividing the factors which
influenced responses to Freud into intrinsic and extrinsic.[15] Among
the extrinsic sources two major ones are those relating to Freud's
national and ethnic affiliations and to the peculiar solidarity of the
psychoanalytic groups.

Several authors (and Freud himself) suggest that anti-semitic feeling
played a role in the hostility incurred by psychoanalysis. This may have
been true of central Europe, but there is little sign of it in the English
literature. The only examples I have noted are two pointed allusions to
Freud as an 'oriental' in American reviews of *The Interpretation of
Dreams*, and a bit of high-spirited nonsense on the subject of circum-
cision from Roy Campbell twenty years later.

On the other hand, Freud did come in for a share of the general
opprobrium of things German which characterised the years during
and immediately after the First World War. Charles Mercier saw Freud
as just a new and more unsavoury addition to the 'monstrous regiment
of German professors that has so long afflicted us'. W. H. B. Stoddart,

14. George Santayana, *The Sense of Beauty* (New York, 1961) p. 53.
15. Shakow and Rapaport, *op. cit.*

one of Freud's earliest British champions, apprehensive in 1915 about 'asking readers to accept as a scientific truth, doctrines which have had their birth in Austria and Germany . . .', disarmed them with the assurance that 'as a matter of fact, Freud himself has no German blood in him, but is a pure Jew'.[16] Christine Ladd-Franklin attributed the more objectionable aspects of psychoanalysis to the fact that 'the German mind is to a certain extent undeveloped when contrasted with the logical and moral sanity of the non-German civilized nations . . . psychoanalysis is most intimately bound up with German kultur.[17]

An article in the *New York Times* contrasted Freud's attitude towards the war unfavourably with that of Karl Kraus. Freud was described as having 'taken up the cudgels for Germany', and exception was taken to his having expressed the hope that 'impartial history will furnish the proof that this very nation in whose language I am writing . . . has sinned least against the laws of human civilisation'. In the immediate post-war atmosphere these unexceptionable sentiments passed for xenophobic ravings and Freud's great essay, 'War and Death' with its moving evocation of 'fellowship in civilisation' was described as 'a little less than a justification of the Prussian theory of the supremacy of the state over morals and ethics'.[18] On the occasion of its translation into English in 1916 the psychiatrist E. E. Southard characterised it as 'a subtle apology for the central powers', and 'an admirable essay in propaganda Teutonica'.

That these remarks were not simply rationalisations of an antecedent antipathy to psychoanalysis is suggested by the fact that at about the same time William Alanson White, whom C. P. Oberndorf describes as one of the 'most effective American propagandists for psychoanalysis',[19] was moved by anti-German feeling to propose that 'the time has come to free American psychiatry from the domination of the Pope at Vienna', and that the American Psychoanalytical Association ought therefore to be dissolved.

Franz Alexander and Sheldon Selesnick have tried to clarify the nature of the opposition Freud provoked by distinguishing between 'psychoanalytic thought' and 'the psychoanalytic movement', their

16. W. H. B. Stoddart, *The New Psychiatry* (London, 1915) p. iv.

17. Christine Ladd-Franklin, 'Freudian Doctrines', *The Nation*, CIII (19 October 1916) p. 373.

18. 'More German than Germans', *New York Times Magazine* (24 August 1919) p. 11.

19. C. P. Oberndorf, *A History of Psychoanalysis in America* (New York, 1964) pp. 135–6.

point being that some of the early opposition to psychoanalysis was due to dubious organisational features of the psychoanalytic associations rather than any wholesale hostility to psychoanalysis itself.[20] They based this view on an exchange of letters between Freud and the distinguished Swiss psychiatrist Eugen Bleuler, one of Freud's earliest non-Viennese adherents, concerning Bleuler's refusal to join the newly constituted International Psychoanalytic Association. Their quotations show that this was due to Bleuler's suspicion that the aims of the new association were medico-political rather than scientific (and not, as Ernest Jones maintained, to Bleuler's sharing his countrymen's proclivity for isolation as evidenced by the Swiss attitude towards international organisations like the United Nations and the League).

One of the episodes which troubled Bleuler was the exclusion of a psychiatrist called Isserlin from attendance at a psychoanalytic meeting because of his persistent criticism. At first Freud dismissed the matter as trifling and countered with the demand that Bleuler should sever his relations with those German psychiatrists who were hostile and derisory. But in a later letter Freud advanced as proof of his open-mindedness his toleration of Adler, who 'is so against my inner convictions that he makes me angry every week. Yet I did not demand his exclusion, his boycott, nor even his decapitation'. (The delightfully Red Queen flavour of this last remark is due to the translators' English rendering; it is safe to assume that Freud was referring to the restraint he had shown in not removing Adler as head of the Vienna Society rather than on not removing Adler's head.)

Bleuler was unpersuaded and persisted in his conviction that 'the introduction of the closed door policy scared away a great many friends and made some of them emotional opponents'. Alexander and Selesnick comment that the Isserlin affair became a kind of test case for the sectarianism of the analytic societies and conclude that 'because of the soundness of its basic concepts and investigative methods, psychoanalysis did not need the dubious help of rigid organisational measures.[21]

20. F. Alexander and S. Selesnick, *Archives of General Psychiatry*, vol. XII (January 1965) pp. 1–9.
21. There is corroboration as to these 'rigid organisational measures' from another source. Max Graf, an early member of Freud's Wednesday circle (and the father of Little Hans) writes: 'Freud ... insisted that ... if one followed Adler and dropped the sexual basis of psychic life, one was no more a Freudian. In short, Freud as the head of the church banished Adler; he ejected him from the official church. Within the space of a few years,

The latter gave at least a nucleus of validity to some of the criticisms
levelled against psychoanalysis.'

According to the received view the answer to the question why
Freud's 'doctrines and methods were found so despicable' lay 'in
Freud's explicit and narrow emphasis on sexuality . . . . To be told
that sexual conflict was the cause of all neurosis and a fear of incest
lay at the bottom of everything was hateful and Freud was duly
hated. . . .'[22]

Ernest Jones spoke in this connection of an 'odium sexicum'. And
there are quite a few recorded responses to Freud which render this
characterisation an apt one. In 1915 Charles Mercier, writing in the
British Medical Journal, characterised psychoanalysis as 'the sedulous
inculcation of obscenity'. The reviewer of Freud's Three Essays on the
Theory of Sexuality for the New York Medical Journal described it as
'pornography gone to seed'. S. Weir Mitchell, the inventor of the
famous 'rest cure', (not to be confused with S. W. Mitchell, an editor
of the British Journal of Medical Psychology and one of Freud's supporters)
threw a book of Freud's into the fire (we are not told which) because
it was 'filthy'.

Boris Sidis, a famous New England psycho-pathologist, made a
violent attack on Freud on this score:

> Psychoanalysis is a conscious and more often a subconscious or unconscious
> debauching of the patient. Nothing is so diabolically calculated to suggest
> sexual perversion as psychoanalysis. Psychoanalysis . . . is a menace to the
> community. . . . Better Christian Science than psychoanalysis![23]

There is no doubt that methodological objections to Freud's claims
were occasionally no more than rationalisations of the shock and revulsion they induced. An illustration is provided by Adolph Wohlgemuth's account of how he went about testing on himself Freud's
assertion of universal bisexuality in men.

> I looked out for and seized opportunities to contemplate at ease and un-
> obtrusively . . . men of all sorts and conditions . . . the martial figure of the

I lived through the whole development of church history: from the first sermons to a
small group of apostles, to the strife between Arius and Athanasius.' 'Reminiscences of
Professor Sigmund Freud', Psychoanalytic Quarterly, XI (1940) p. 473.

22. Lancelot Law Whyte, The Unconscious Before Freud (New York, 1960) pp. 167–8.

23. Boris Sidis, Symptomatology, Psychognosis and Diagnosis of Psychopathic Disease.
Boston, 1914) p. vii.

dashing soldier or the brainy and intellectual countenance of the thinker, the athlete, or the delicate and dreamy artist – all men who would probably please and whose exterior decidedly attracted me. I contemplated them and dwelt upon their personal advantages, having constantly in mind the purpose of the experiment. I imagined the preliminary period of a sexual approach; but I think it unnecessary to enter here into further details of this process, and will state at once the result of these experiments. I have been unable to come across the least trace of any homosexual propensity in my experiences.[24]

The reasoning on the basis of which Wohlgemuth was persuaded to submit himself to this ordeal is worth retrieving, if only to illustrate that the production of arguments which defy parody was not a monopoly of the Freudians.

... When looking at a woman and indulging in sexual phantasies it is a well-known fact that, with the normal man, the impulse of contrectation (i.e. touching), to use Moll's term, occurs. From this I reasoned that a similar experience must occur in the homosexually disposed individual with regard to another male. If, therefore, I were to indulge in such phantasies, whilst contemplating a man, as would cause an impulse to contrectation when practised with respect to a woman, I, as a trained observer, should certainly be able to detect any incipient conative tendencies and affective experiences, if they be present.

Nor did so rigorous an experimentalist as Wohlgemuth neglect to control for the possibility that his failure 'to detect any incipient conative tendencies and affective experiences' might evidence a general enfeeblement rather than the absence of specifically homosexual inclinations. Recalling ungallantly that 'a great number of women exert ... a repulsive affect ...' he reasoned that

if such women are made the object of similar experiments as those described above with men, and if in spite of the primary repulsion, sexual conative tendencies, an incipient libido, be detected to be present, such a fact would certainly tend to prove my introspection reliable ... I chose then as suitable subjects for these experiments ... old and decrepit women, and such as were afflicted with some nauseating complaint, women of varying degrees of cleanliness, or rather uncleanliness. In all these cased I have invariably been able to discover decidedly sexual conative tendencies and unmistakable libido ... I have, therefore no hesitation whatever in affirming that Freud's statement, that there are homosexual tendencies in every man at some time or another, to be a groundless assertion.

24. A. Wohlgemuth, *A Critical Examination of Psychoanalysis* (London, 1923) pp. 157–9.

Though Wolgemuth's self-experiment constitutes one of the most engaging episodes in the martyrology of science, it is otherwise worthless. As Wohlgemuth himself conceded in his reply to J. C. Flugel's criticisms, 'My argument does not touch the real point at issue'.

The bad arguments which Freud occasionally provoked tempted Freudians to the convenient inference that all the methodological objections by which they were plagued sprang from a reluctance to acknowledge the truth of their claims and could be ignored. But at the same time that Freud and his advocates were invoking the revulsion produced by his emphasis on sexuality to account for the opposition which he met, critics of psychoanalysis were plaintively demanding how mere rational argument could be expected to make headway against doctrines so alluring.

Bernard Sachs, for example, wrote: 'It is the sex appeal of Freudian doctrines that has given psychoanalytic writing their great vogue among literary and professional people.'[25]

At about the same time Robert Woodworth attributed 'the popular interest in psychoanalysis ... largely to the freedom with which Freud and his disciples have handled the problem of sex.'[26]

Italo Svevo, who combines mockery of the pretensions of psychoanalysis with mockery of its disparagers in proportions which it is difficult to assess, has the hero of *The Confessions of Zeno* (1922) reflect:

> ... They have found out what was the matter with me. The diagnosis is exactly the same as the one that Sophocles drew up long ago for poor Oedipus: I was in love with my mother and wanted to murder my father ... I listened enraptured. It was a disease that exalted me to a place among the great ones of the earth; a disease so dignified that it could trace back its pedigree even to the mythological age.

But there were more creditable reasons for being favourably impressed by Freud's emphasis on man's instinctual nature. William Morton Wheeler, a distinguished zoologist, in a paper read at Harvard in 1917, scornfully contrasted academic psychologists who 'merely hint at the existence of such stupendous and fundamental biological phenomena as those of hunger, sex, and fear ... and whose works ... read as if they had been composed by beings that had been born and

25. Bernard Sachs, 'Bumke's Critique of Psychoanalysis', *Mental Hygiene* (July 1932) p. 409.
26. Robert Woodworth, *A Quarter Century of Learning* (New York, 1931) p. 140.

bred in a belfry, castrated in early infancy, and fed continually for
fifty years through a tube with a stream of liquid nutriment of constant chemical composition' with the psychoanalysts who 'have had the
courage to dig up the subconscious, that hotbed of all the egotism,
greed, lust, pugnacity, cowardice, sloth, hate and envy which every
single one of us carries about as his inheritance from the animal world.'[27]

This indictment was endorsed, though less colourfully, by at least
one academic psychologist. L. L. Thurstone in a symposium on the
contribution of 'Freudism' to psychology conceded the 'gross defi-
ciencies in the subject matter of psychology' to which psychoanalysts
had called attention.

> They are constantly searching for the relation between the fundamental
> cravings and wants of people and the ways in which these wants are expressed
> and satisfied . . . and that relation is more important as a determinant of
> personality and conduct, than the stimulus-response relation to which we
> scientific psychologists have given most of our effort.[28]

Another set of objections centred about the supposed immoral
therapeutic and prophylactic implications of Freud's theory of the
neuroses. It was asserted that analysts prescribed intercourse as a therapeutic measure; that, in any case, the effect of the treatment was to
alienate the patient from the prevailing sexual code, and that analysts
had sexual relations with their patients.

A reviewer in the *British Medical Journal* warned that psychoanalytic
therapy 'contains an element of danger for the patient who . . . may
receive advice from her psychoanalytic physician repugnant to the
ordinary code of morality.'[29]

Bernard Sachs claimed that 'the good affects of psychoanalytic
therapy have been heralded by patients because they have been encouraged, if not ordered, to violate the prevailing code of morality.'
This sounds like an agreeable fantasy but, in fact, it was more than
that. Whatever the practice of analysts may have been, it is certain
that there were physicians who did recommend intercourse to their
patients and that some of these did so on what they took to be Freud's
authority.

27. W. M. Wheeler, 'On Instincts', *Journal of Abnormal Psychology*, xv, nos 5–6 (December 1920 – March 1921) p. 316.
28. L. L. Thurstone, 'Influence of Freudism on Theoretical Psychology', *The Psychological Review*, xxi, no. 3 (May 1924) p. 180.
29. *British Medical Journal* (5 July 1913) p. 24.

Freud's apprehensiveness about this trend caused him to denounce it as 'wild psychoanalysis' in a paper of 1910, which, however, leaves an exaggerated impression as to the extent to which the prophylactic and therapeutic value of intercourse was an unwarranted inference from Freud's writings. A careful reading of Freud's paper, which was often cited to refute those who understood Freud to hold that sexual abstinence was in itself pathogenic, and which Brill was careful to include in the second edition of *Selected Papers in Hysteria*, shows that the mistake made by the physician, who was the subject of Freud's remonstrance, was not that he had misunderstood Freud, but that he had misdiagnosed his patient, confounding an anxiety-hysteria with an anxiety-neurosis; the right treatment but the wrong illness, as it were.

Pierre Janet in an address to the International Congress of Psychiatry in 1913 drew the implication that Freud's explanation of the neuroses committed him to holding that a visit to a brothel would have as much therapeutic effect as psychoanalytic sessions. This provoked Ernest Jones to accuse him of deliberate, malicious prevarication. But it is more likely that Janet was merely guilty of carelessly confounding Freud's aetiology of the 'actual' neuroses with that of the psychoneuroses, thus erroneously extending to the latter the pathogenic role Freud had assigned to sexual abstinence in the former.

But the accusation that Freud and his followers 'corrupted' their patients had a source more difficult to allay than simple misunderstanding of the distinction between the actual and the psychoneuroses in doubts as to the correctness, and sometimes even as to the candour, of Freud's theory of sublimation.

Paul Bjerre, a Swedish analyst, raised this issue in his book *The History and Practice of Psychoanalysis*. If, he asked, a sexual desire always lies at the base of a neurosis how can merely psychic treatment work? 'It is very easy to suspect that analysts might . . . advise sexual congress as a cure for neuroses.' Bjerre went on to say that some analysts, in fact, did so but that 'Freud holds aloof from them' in consequence.[30]

It is thus understandable that a common inference from Freud's writing should have been, as one indignant critic put it, that 'absolute continence is unnatural and incompatible with mental health'.[31]

30. P. Bjerre, *The History and Practice of Psychoanalysis* (Boston, 1916) p. 138.
31. G. M. Cullen, 'Psychoanalysis Attacked', *The Living Age* (1921).

A character in an Aldous Huxley short story of the same period remarks to another that it is better that she should have sexual thrills than repressions. 'Read Freud. Repressions are the devil.'

The *New York Times* found it necessary to contradict this misconception editorially:

> ... While it is true that the Freudians teach that many mental, and some physical, ills are the result of 'repressions', they seek the cure for these ills not in 'Do as you please', but in turning the repressed energies to high and proper uses – 'sublimation', they call it. Whoever does anything else – who finds in psychoanalysis license instead of liberty – is not a follower of Freud ... but a charlatan, certainly ignorant and probably vicious.[32]

Whereas the *New York Times* accepted Freud's doctrine of sublimation at its face value some shared Jung's view that the notion of sublimation was 'a pious wish structure invented for the quieting of inopportune questioners'. Jung's suspicion with regard to sublimation is dramatised in Thomas Mann's *The Magic Mountain*, in the comments of Hofrat Behrens, the director of the sanitarium:

> ... This cursed *libido*! ... We have psychoanalysis, we give the noodles every chance to talk themselves out – much good it does them! The more they talk the more lecherous they get. I preach mathematics ... I tell them that if they will occupy themselves with the study of mathematics they will find in it the best remedy against the lusts of the flesh. Lawyer Paravant was a bad case; he took my advice, he is now busy squaring the circle, and gets great relief. But most of them are too witless and lazy, God help them.[33]

No account of the sources of the hostility towards psychoanalysis would be complete which failed to mention the trepidation aroused by the psychoanalytic notion of the 'transference'. It was the transference, the aim, as Freud put it, 'of attaching the patient to the person of the physician', which provoked one critic to ask rhetorically, 'Who after learning of this would submit his young daughter to psychoanalysis?' A reviewer in the *British Medical Journal* was content to issue a friendly warning:

32. *New York Times* (29 March 1921) p. 14, col. 5.

33. With characteristic perspicacity Mann has discerned Freud's own, at least intermittent, view of the matter. Sentiments similar to those of Hofrat Behrens are expressed by Freud in a letter to Pfister of January 1909, in which he states that since sublimation is 'too difficult for most patients our cure generally issues in the search for gratification'. Ernest Jones, *Sigmund Freud: Life and Work*, Vol. 2, (London, 1958) p. 489.

.... The situation contains elements of danger for the professional reputation of the psychoanalyst, and it would not be prudent for him to neglect any of those precautions usually observed by members of the profession in the clinical examination of hysterical women.[34]

Much of the anti-psychoanalytic literature of the time is prone to somewhat coy innuendoes as to the kind of relationship between the patient and his physician which the practice of transference encouraged. For example, Bernard Sachs remarked: 'We all know the mischief that has been wrought by this whole transference business. And as far as the patient's emotional reactions to the psychoanalyst are concerned, the less said the better.[35] (In his *A History of Psychoanalysis in America*, C. P. Oberndorf records that this was a common accusation and tells of a quick-witted woman he was analysing who, when warned that analysts have sexual relations with their patients, replied, 'Poor Dr Oberndorf, he sees six patients a day.')

Joseph Jastrow wrote:

> I cannot close my eyes nor those of the reader to the disquieting tales of the abuse of the relation of analyst-patient ... in which the transference eased the way of abuse ... remember that not all analysts are saints and the rest can be left to the reader's imagination.[36]

What Jastrow was content to leave to his readers' imagination was made explicit by Gilbert Seldes in his book *Can Such Things Be* (New York, 1931), to which Jastrow referred them. Seldes relates stories of 'the translation of the verbal intimacy which the method involved into physical intimacy between practitioners and patients'. One concerns 'a handsome American matron' who left her husband to have an affair with her Viennese analyst. 'The husband bought a hussar's whip and matched a duelling scar on the psychoanalyst's cheek with half a dozen welts, until the whip broke. He returned to America and got a divorce and the custody of his three children.' As for the woman, Seldes relates that the member of the American Medical Association of Vienna who told him the story 'saw her himself not so long ago at the races in Baden-Baden – a heavily rouged and powdered travesty of her formerly wholesomely alluring self in company with a notorious South American profligate.' Though some today might regard this story as

34. *British Medical Journal*, op. cit.
35. Sachs, *Mental Hygiene*.
36. Joseph Jastrow, *The House That Freud Built* (New York, 1959) p. 238.

inadvertent testimony to the regenerative powers of psychoanalytic treatment, we can be sure Seldes' American readers, for whom consorting with a South American was half way towards miscegenation, would not have seen it in this light.

But what is significant about Seldes' remarks in their bearing on Freud's standing at the time is the pains which he takes to contrast the 'irresponsible practitioners' of his anecdotes with the 'leaders of the science themselves' who 'were the simplest and most honest of men.' One of the subtitles of the chapter on psychoanalysis runs 'While real scientists perfect theories to benefit mankind, quacks practise on Americans!' – the 'real scientists' being Freud and those for whom he vouched.

There were three major methodological criticisms of Freud. These were that Freud took no precautions against suggesting aetiologies to his patients, that his methods of interpretation were arbitrary, and that he abused the term sexual and its cognates. Of those, the most frequently iterated was the charge of suggestion. This may have been felt to have particular weight since Freud's seduction error was sometimes attributed to it.

A neurologist writing in *Brain* in 1911 objected to 'the so-called facts of psychoanalysis' that

> 'we may put into (the patient's) mind just what we want to find there. We know that Freud gave up that portion of his theory which relates to sexual assaults, because he found that his patients had misled him. And if the master of this method may be decieved, how much more his disciples?[37]

That Freud's replies to these misgivings (for example in the twenty-eighth of the *Introductory Lectures*) were not found convincing is indicated by the fact that almost two decades later Bernard Hart, one of Freud's earliest sympathisers, repeated the objection in his *Psychopathology: Its Development and Its Place in Medicine* (London, 1928):

> The preconceptions of the analyst, the particular moments at which he sees fit to intervene in the patient's narrative, the emphasis which he directs to certain features of the narrative, the point at which he deems the flow of associations to have reached the significant element, all these are abundantly able to produce decided alterations in the subsequent functioning of the patient's mind.

37. J. A. Ormerod, 'Two Theories of Hysteria', *Brain*, XXXIII (January 1911) p. 287.

In one of the earliest assessments of Freud to be published in the United States, J. J. Putnam, later to be one of Freud's staunchest American advocates, objected that

...When the physician is fully imbued with the belief in the sexual origin of the patient's illness, he must, by virtue of the closeness of this relationship, be in a position to impress his view, unconsciously, upon his patients, and might easily draw from them an acquiescence and an endorsement which would not in reality be as spontaneous as it seemed.[38]

But Putnam came to feel, after further experience with Freud's method, that his original objections and apprehensions were unfounded. Others retained their misgivings. And still others came to feel the force of these objections after having initially discounted them (for example, Frederick Peterson, Boris Sidis, Samuel Tannenbaum and, most notoriously, Jung).

Another frequent source of misgiving was the impression of arbitrariness produced by Freud's interpretative procedures and by his employment of symbolism in particular. In 1912 an American psychologist, Frederick Lyman Wells, referred to symbolism as 'the phase of psychoanalysis to which the most legitimate objections are raised'.[39]

'There is absolutely nothing in the universe which may not readily be made into a sexual symbol,' objected Knight Dunlap, a professor of psychology and author of the first book explicitly devoted to the refutation of psychoanalytic claims.

...All natural and artificial objects can be turned into Freudian symbols. We may explain, by Freudian principles, why trees have their roots in the ground; why we write with pens; why we put a quart of wine into a bottle instead of hanging it on hooks like a ham; and so on.[40]

The psychiatrist Pearce Bailey was less witty but blunter: 'Freud and his industrious followers... make symbols mean what they like.'[41]

In 1925 Aldous Huxley, writing in an American journal, confided that

38. J. J. Putnam, 'Recent Experiences as the Study and Treatment of Hysteria at the Massachusetts General Hospital; with Remarks on Freud's Method of Treatment by "Psychoanalysis"', *Journal of Abnormal Psychology*, vol. 1 (April 1906) pp. 40–1.
39. F. L. Wells, 'Review of Psychoanalysis; its Themes and Applications' by A. A. Brill, *Journal of Abnormal Psychology*, vol. 7 (1912–13) p. 447.
40. Knight Dunlap, 'The Pragmatic Advantage of Freudo-analysis', *Psychoanalytic Review*, 1 (1913) p. 151.
41. P. Bailey, 'Hero Myths According to Freud', *New Republic* (13 March 1915) p. 161.

it was the machinery of symbolism, by which the analyst transforms the manifest into the latent dream content, that shook any faith I might possibly have had in the system. It seemed to me, as I read those lists of symbols and those obscene allegorical interpretations of simple dreams, that I had seen this sort of thing before. I remembered, for example, that old-fashioned interpretation of the Song of Solomon ... I had never, even in infancy, whole-heartedly believed that the amorous damsel in the Song of Songs was, prophetically, the Church and her lover the Saviour. Why should I then accept as valid the symbolism invented by Dr. Freud? There are no better reasons for believing that walking upstairs or flying are dream equivalents of fornication than for believing that the girl in the Song of Solomon is the Church of Christ.[42]

Many comments on Freud's deployment of his sexual terminology manifest the irritated bewilderment Hans Castorp felt towards Dr Krokowski's lectures on psychoanalysis.

... The speaker employed the word 'love' in a somewhat ambiguous sense so that you were never quite sure where you were with it, or whether he had reference to its sacred, or its passionate and fleshly aspect – and this doubt gave one a slightly seasick feeling.[43]

But often it was neither the mere breadth of Freud's notion of sexuality nor its concertina-like character which was found troubling, but the suspicion, as Freud himself put it, that his 'unwarrantable expansion' of the term sexual 'was in order that (my) assertion regarding the sexual origin of the neuroses and the sexual significance of symptoms might be maintained' (last paragraph of the twentieth of the *Introductory Lectures*). For example, the psychotherapist, Dr T. A. Ross spoke of a 'certain equivocation' on the part of Freudians:

The statement is made by them that sex is at the bottom of every neurosis, and when people hold up their hands at this statement, the further statement is made that by sex they mean all sorts of manifestations of love ... that, in short, the term sex for the Freudian is a much wider one than for other people. And yet when one comes to the case material which has been given frequently in great detail in the Freudian literature, one finds that the sex manifestations there described are just what anyone else would call sex manifestations.[44]

42. Aldous Huxley, 'Is Psychoanalysis a Science?', *The Forum*, LXXIII (1925) pp. 316–17.
43. Thomas Mann, *The Magic Mountain* (London, 1960) p. 130.
44. T. A. Ross, *An Introduction to Analytical Psychotherapy* (New York, 1932) p. 82.

The same complaint was made by a member of the influential group
of Philadelphia neurologists:

When anyone now accuses the disciples of the newer psychology of laying
greater stress on sexual matters as a cause of mental trouble than they deserve,
the work 'libido' is claimed to be used symbolically . . . I refuse to make
charges of bad faith, but I do not think the disciples of Freudism are altogether frank in their statements as to their use of the word. I think their
enthusiasm has made them a little disingenuous. The present explanation
was not given till adverse criticism had been made.[45]

That there was some warrant for this suspicion may be inferred from
a sample of the elucidations of the sexual theory proferred by Freud's
expositors. One of them observed:

Many have strongly objected to Freud's theory principally on account of
the term 'sexual', translating it for themselves to mean sexual in the narrowest
sense. . . . Rather does it embrace life and love and creation, indeed, the
whole diffused tendency to seek expression, starting with mother-love and
graduating to the power to not only create life but to be capable of any
creative work.[46]

Another argued that:

The meaning of sexual manifestations in the Freudian sense . . . covers a
broad and comprehensive field of activity, whether bodily desires or mental
longings. It embraces all desires, instincts, wishes, ambitions – like hunger,
sex, acquisition, aspiration, the social sense, love of art, etc. This is a far cry
from the narrow vulgar conception of the term which seems to be understood by the men opposing the Freudian psychology.[47]

Nor can it be said that these equivocations were restricted to ill-
informed or faint-hearted apologists. It was a founder-member of
the New York Psychoanalytic Society who explained that psychoanalysis used the word sex 'in so broad a sense that even the most
puritan minded need not be startled . . . without any implication
necessarily of any moral unfitness or physical grossness'. And Ernest
Jones himself, in the original preface of his book *Papers on Psycho-*

45. Charles W. Burr, 'A Criticism of Psychoanalysis', *American Journal of Insanity*,
LXXI, no. 2 (October 1914) p. 244.
46. *The Medical Record*, LXXXIV (9 August 1913) p. 258.
47. *Journal of the American Medical Association* (28 March 1914) p. 1036.

analysis, elucidated Freud's conception of sexual instinct in terms of its affinity to 'Schopenhauer's and Nietzsche's "Wille Zur Machte", Bergson's "Elan Vital", Shaw's "Life Force", and the "vital impulse" of so many writers all of which,' Jones concluded, 'are equivalent to what Freud termed "Libido"'.[48] And yet, a few years later, Jones was authoritatively defining libido as 'nothing less than sexual hunger'. No wonder Hans Castorp felt sea-sick!

Another feature of Freud's work often selected for comment war what may loosely be termed his explanatory style. However, these were radical divergences as to what this explanatory style amounted to, what its affinities were. Some found these in mechanistic physics or biology, others in teleology and animism. There was ample warrant in Freud's writings themselves for either assimilation.

The philosopher, Paul Carus, contrasting Schopenhauer's animistic account of gravitation in terms of the stone's will to fall with Freud's explanations, observed that whereas

some philosophers take features typical of the highest and most complicated forms of existence and generalise them to explain the nature of lower forms. Others do the reverse, they generalise the lowest forms and explain all higher features as mere repetition of simpler modes of activity . . . Freud generalises the lower . . . so as to cover the higher.[49]

On the other hand, *Harper's Weekly* found in Freud's views 'a great advance on the hopeless materialistic stand-point of the doctors of a quarter of a century ago . . . Freud lays great stress on the purpose underlying neurotic reactions.'[50] Neither view can be written off as just a popular misunderstanding. A New York analyst writing in a medical journal in 1915 contrasted the contemporary medical mind 'brought up in the school of the natural sciences, saturated with mechanistic explanations' and predisposed to 'what metaphysicians designate as materialism' with 'the practice of psychoanalysis (which) demands the idealistic view'.[51]

To an extent the contradiction is only apparent. Someone who was

48. Ernest Jones, *Papers on Psychoanalysis* (London 1913) p. xi. This account of libido was deleted from subsequent editions.

49. Paul Carus, 'Wrong Generalisations in Philosophy: Schopenhauer and Freud', *The Monist*, XXIII (1913) p. 150.

50. *Harper's Weekly* (24 June 1911) p. 6.

51. Mary Isham, 'Some Implications of Psychoanalysis', *New York Medical Journal* (21 August 1915) p. 390.

struck by the contrast between Freud's emphasis on the influence of
mental conflict on the disposition to neurotic illness and the theories
of hereditary degeneracy held by some of Freud's contemporaries
might mark this awareness by characterising Freud's views as 'idealistic'; while those who were struck rather by the biological or carnal
nature of the impulses in question might use the same term to charac-
terise the mental-moralistic views which Freud also supplanted.[52]

This, however, did not exhaust the sources of ambiguity. There
remained the question of how Freud conceived these pathogenic
wishes to exert their influence. Though the explanatory factors which
Freud invoked might be in some sense 'materialistic', their mode of
operation was often characterised in animistic idioms: it is as if an itch
were to be credited with both the inclination and the ability to scratch
itself.

Among those who were struck rather by this aspect of Freud's
explanations was Sidney Hook who felt that since 'the unconscious
works more intelligently to attain its ends than does ever active intelligence ... Freud's unconscious is in line with the elan vital of Bergson,
the super-empirical entelechies of Driesch and the 'soul spook' of
McDougall....[53]

The authors of a history of science, summing up the controversy
over the theory of evolution, write:

> Those who had external reasons for wishing to rebut the new doctrine
> tended to exaggerate the technical objections, flogging the genuine diffi-
> culties still facing the theory of evolution for more than they were worth:
> meanwhile, Darwin's henchmen were tempted in return to play down these
> difficulties in public, for fear of giving prejudiced objectors too much of a
> foothold.[54]

With the qualification that it is still an open question just how much
the technical objections to Freud were worth and that Freud's advocates
have not been dead long enough to be designated 'henchmen', their

52. 'The psychiatric schools of thought that predominated between the period of the
decline of the Nancy school of suggestion (c. 1890) and the rise of the psychoanalytical
school (1910) were chiefly rationalistic, moral, exhortative, and re-educational. They
appealed to the reason of the patient, to his conscious thinking and feeling.' Iago Galdston,
Progress in Medicine (New York, 1940) pp. 260–1.

53. S. Hook, 'Marxism, Metaphysics and Modern Science', *The Modern Quarterly*,
IV (1927) p. 389.

54. Stephen Toulmin and June Goodfield, *The Discovery of Time* (London, 1967) p. 259.

account fits equally well the controversy over the empirical warranta-
bility of Freud's theories.

But there is a striking feature of Freud's role in our lives to which
the controversial literature over his contribution to psychopathology
does not do justice – the feature which provoked Alfred Kazin to
remark that

> psychoanalytical literature has replaced the Bible as the place to which
> people turn for an explanation of their suffering, and a source of consolation.[55]

And the feature which is ironically noted in Thomas Mann's account
of Dr Krokowski's lectures:

> ... With open arms he summoned all and sundry to come unto him.
> 'Come unto me,' he was saying, though not in those words, 'come unto me,
> all ye who are weary and heavy laden.' And he left no doubt of his conviction
> that all those present *were* weary and heavy laden. He spoke of secret suffer-
> ing, of shame and sorrow, of the redeeming power of the analytic.

We find it in Hans Sachs' remark that reading *The Interpretation of
Dreams* was 'the moment of destiny' for him: ... 'when I had finished
the book I had found the one thing worthwhile for me to live for;
many years later I discovered that it was the only thing I could live
by.'[56] The same note of exaltation sounds in a remark Jung addressed
to Freud in the early years of their association – 'to know your science
means to have eaten from the Tree of Paradise'. And in Theodore
Dreiser's comparison of Freud to 'a conqueror who has taken a city,
entered its age-old hoary prisons, there generously proceeding to
release from their gloomy and rusted cells the prisoners of formulae,
faith and illusions which have wracked and worn man for hundreds
and thousands of years.'[57]

In a paragraph in which he discusses his relation to Nietzsche,
Dostoievsky and Freud, André Gide speaks of having found in Freud
'rather an authorisation than an awakening. Above all (he) taught me to
cease doubting myself, to cease fearing my thoughts, and to let those
thoughts lead me to those lands that were not after all uninhabitable
since I found (him) already there.'[58]

55. Alfred Kazin, 'The Freudian Revolution Analysed', *Freud and the Twentieth Century*,
ed. Benjamin Nelson (London, 1958) p. 15.
56. Hans Sachs, *Freud: Master and Friend* (Cambridge, Mass., 1944) p. 1.
57. Theodore Drieser, 'Remarks', *Psychoanalytic Review* (July 1931) p. 250.
58. André Gide, *Pretexts* (London, 1959) p. 306.

These remarks suggest that a potent source of Freud's 'redeeming power' is his skill in easing what G. K. Chesterton, in an essay on Freud, called 'our monstrous burden of secrecy'.[59]

George Orwell has left a vivid record of the liberating effect this sort of realisation can have:

> ... Now and again [he wrote] there appears a writer who opens up a new world not by revealing what is strange but by revealing what is familiar. ... Here is a world of stuff which you supposed to be of its nature incommunicable, and somebody has managed to communicate it. The effect is to break down, at any rate momentarily, the solitude in which the human being lives.[60]

Though Orwell was referring to James Joyce's *Ulysses* his words are strikingly evocative of what many have felt towards Freud. And they suggest an answer to D. H. Lawrence's dismissive view that once we have gotten over the excitement of realising 'how thrillingly immoral things really are', we will forget the concepts of psychoanalysis 'as we have forgotten so many other catch words' and will once again be 'just where we were'.[61]

There is good reason to think that we shall never again be where we were; that though the extent, and even the precise character, of Freud's 'scientific' achievement will remain a matter of dispute for some time to come, what is not disputable is that Freud broke down, and not just momentarily, one of the solitudes in which we lived.

59. G. K. Chesterton, 'The Game of Psychoanalysis', *Century*, CVI (1923) p. 38.
60. George Orwell, 'Inside the Whale', *Selected Essays* (London, 1957) pp. 11–12.
61. D. H. Lawrence, *Fantasia of the Unconscious* (London, 1961) p. 126.

JACQUES RIVIÈRE

The Three Main Theses of Psychoanalysis (1924)

EACH time I undertake a series of lectures, I vow formally to lay aside all oratorical preliminaries. Once again I have made this vow. However, I cannot bring myself to go directly to my subject without justifying it in a few words and especially without first telling you my thoughts about it.

I shall admit naïvely that I find my subject both delicate and extremely interesting. The fact that it has been almost completely unexplored, at least from the point of view from which I intend to treat it, acts both in its favours and against it

There is, especially in foreign languages, an enormous body of literature on Freud which I do not know. The most lamentable death of Marcel Proust has already given rise to numerous articles; the January 1st issue of the *Nouvelle Revue Française* alone contains about fifty.

In spite of this, my subject, as I understand it, continues to seem to me to be entirely unexplored, and this fact both encourages and intimidates me.

It intimidates me because I am not very certain of where I am going and because I feel that I have no chance of arriving at definitive affirmations.

I perceive a quantity of ideas to be brought up, studied, and traced; but I am somewhat like a mining engineer who, in the depths of a mine, wonders what veins are going to yield, what galleries must be cut, which ones will keep him in the seam the longest. Of one thing only am I certain: I shall come to dead ends. I shall have to retrace my steps at times, and I shall perhaps merely touch upon the main point while I get entangled in the inessential. It will certainly happen that I shall say things to you that will appear less true to me as soon as I have said them, things that I shall have to withdraw or change.

I beg you to excuse me. These mishaps to which I shall expose you with a heart that you may call very light, are the ransom of the extreme importance, the extreme richness and the extreme originality of the subject we are tackling. If Proust has proved one thing, it is that nothing can take the place of time. And this is more true in the field of ideas than in any other field. The ideas that we are going to bring up have not as yet undergone that influence of the years which alone, like a slow sun, can ripen them. I am not to be blamed. With some presumption, perhaps, but also with some justification, I claim that the hesitations and perhaps the marking of time that will accompany this study we are undertaking together, are inevitable and should not be imputed to me as a crime.

But it is time to define, at least in general terms, this subject which is so new and so admirable and which will gain me your forbearance.

As you may well think, I do not intend to exhaust all that can be said about Freud and Proust. No, I intend to study them from a specific point of view. Roughly, I should like to study what is new in their contribution to psychology. I should like to determine what progress they can cause us to make in the knowledge of that which the classical age called the human heart. (I beg you to give the word heart its most general meaning.)

This progress can be of two kinds: it can consist of the acquisition of new feelings, new sensations, new levels of consciousness, or of the invention of new methods for exploring the latter, the invention of a new way of tackling feelings and sensations. We shall make a distinction between these two kinds of progress, but not with such rigidity as to deny ourselves points of view which might arise and cancel this difference.

One further remark. Our study will not be a simple exposition. You must not expect to leave these talks with a knowledge of the systems of Freud and Proust, as one leaves a course at the Sorbonne knowing the systems of Plato. I shall try to extract from the systems of our two authors (if, indeed, they have any) only what can be linked to and clarified by our personal experience.

Freud has been taken to task by Jules Romains among others for a certain scientific levity, that is, for a certain tendency to transform his hypotheses into laws without having gathered the quantity of experiments and objective proof that would give him the right to do so.

With two scientific ideas [says Jules Romains], he does not hesitate to announce one of those 'brilliant points of view' which, to be sure, indicate a great intellectual activity and which one would like to call the work of a genius, but they cannot be classified later in the same part of the mind as good scientific money. They are paper money bound up with the destiny of the bank which issues them.

In many passages, however, Freud gives proof of quite a noticeable carefulness and even takes the trouble to point out himself the gaps in his theory and the points at which experimentation has not yet confirmed its truth. In the *Introduction to Psychoanalysis* he writes: The answer to this question does not seem urgent to me and especially it is not certain enough for anyone to attempt to formulate it. Let us allow the progress of scientific work to go on and let us wait patiently.' On the threshold of a tempting generalisation of an idea which he has just uttered, he remarks: 'However, the psychoanalytic explanation of neuroses has no connection with considerations of such vast import.'

He always examines the objections which are presented to him with a great deal of care. For example, in the last chapter of the *Introduction to Psychoanalysis*, we find a remarkable discussion of the idea that all the discoveries of psychoanalysis might be merely the result of suggestions made to the patients. When we think of the importance of this objection and note the masterly way in which Freud answers it, we feel an impression of confidence both in his honesty and in his intellectual power.

However, it must be admitted that there is something to the criticism of Jules Romains, and that there are certain errors in the method of Freud of which we must absolutely be forewarned, errors which we must take into consideration before we set off to follow him.

It is evident that we are dealing with an extremely alive and active imagination which sometimes reacts a little too quickly to the first indications of an experiment. When we read Freud, we are struck by the rapidity of certain of his conclusions. Very often we see him making an affirmation which he has immediately generalised from a single fact that he reports; very often, too, if *he is able* to interpret a fact along the lines of theory, he seems to find this sufficient to exclude any other interpretation.

On the other hand, the undeniable victory of his central idea over the enigmas of nature creates a sort of intoxication in him which leads him to imperialism. I mean that he tries to annex too many phenomena to his explanation. In particular, his interpretation of dreams and slips, filled with profound observations, seems to me much more artificial on the whole, and much less convincing, than his theory of neurosis. And when I learn that chronologically he began by an explanation of neurotic symptoms, I wonder if his whole theory of dreams and slips is not a somewhat arbitrary, or at least a too systematic, extension of an accurate idea into a domain that could not accept it, at least in its textual form.

In other words, I wonder if the order – Slips, Dreams, Neuroses – that Freud has chosen for the exposition of his theory in *Introduction to Psychoanalysis* is not extremely specious; I wonder if it does not risk falsifying the true movement of his mind in the course of his discoveries, as well as the very value of these discoveries. Even if it seems logical to show the unconscious at work first in the most simple actions of normal, daily life, this procedure becomes an error in method if the presence of the unconscious cannot be demonstrated with as much proof in these acts as in pathological acts, if its intervention is more debatable in the former than in the latter, if, in fact, its presence was not first divulged in the former.

In vain I try. The theory of slips and dreams is to me like a double portico constructed later by Freud in front of the monument he had raised. He thinks it may give a more pleasing and convincing approach to the monument; but in my opinion he is mistaken because, in this first part, we do not have a strong enough impression of being in contact with an irrefutable, invincible experience, the one which gave rise to the theory. We sense the subtlety of the author, but we do not feel his reasons clearly enough.

That is why I think we must keep our eye mainly on his theory of neuroses if we want to grasp his thought at its point of maximum intent, if we want to recognise all the consequences it implies, all the generalisations of which it is capable, its greatest extent, or rather, its greatest explosive force.

In what follows, I do not want to analyse the Freudian doctrine in detail, but on the contrary, assuming that my readers know it, I should like to show its virtuality, if I may use this word. I want to present the three great psychological discoveries for which we are indebted to Freud and to show what an extraordinary light they can infuse into the study of inner facts and, especially, feelings. I particularly want to make you feel how extensible these discoveries are, what form they can assume that will be even more flexible and generous, as it were, an the one Freud gave them.

In the account of the facts which suggested to him the first idea of his theory – they were, as is well known, the total manifestations of hysteria – Freud emphasised very strongly the complete ignorance of his patients as to the causes and aims of the actions they were accomplishing; he wrote:

> While she was carrying out the compulsive act, the patient was ignorant of its 'meaning' in respect both to its origin and its aim. Psychological processes were going on within her, processes which had produced the compulsive act. Through her normal psychological set-up, she clearly perceived the product, but none of the psychological circumstances had reached her conscious mind. . . . We are thinking of such situations when we speak of *unconscious psychological processes.*[1]

And Freud concludes:

> In these symptoms of compulsive neuroses, in these images and compulsions which rise up from some undetermined place and seem so refractory to all the influences of normal life, which seem even to the patient to be *all-powerful guests from another world, immortals coming and mixing with the tumult of mortal life*, how can we not recognize the sign of a particular psychological region, isolated from the rest, from all the other activities and manifestations of inner life? These symptoms, images, and compulsions lead us unmistakably to the conviction of the existence of a psychological unconscious.[2]

At first there does not seem to be anything unusually new in these passages, and it may well seem paradoxical that we claim to see one of the sublimities of Freudian theory in them. The unconscious is not a Freudian discovery. Names will probably be mentioned right away that will seem to reduce his originality on this point to the slimmest proportions: names as early as that of Leibnitz, then the names of Schopenhauer, Hartmann, Bergson, and many others.

However, I answer:

1. That there is a considerable difference between a metaphysical and a psychological concept of the unconscious; that admitting the existence of the unconscious as a principle, as a force, as an entity, is quite different from admitting its existence as a body of facts, a group of phenomena.

2. That in reality many contemporary psychologists, especially Pierre Janet and his school, still refuse to admit the existence of a psychological unconscious.

3. Finally, assuming that the psychological unconscious is recognised by everyone as a kingdom, a domain, Freud is the first to conceive of it:

a. As a domain or a definite realm with a fixed geography, or, to speak without metaphor, as containing tendencies, extremely precise impulses, directed towards special ends.

b. As a domain or a realm that can be explored starting from the conscious mind and that even must be explored if the latter is to be understood.

At this point I regain enough confidence to state that this seems to me to be completely original and extremely important. Just think that up to now consciousness has been conceived of as a closed room in which there were, as if inscribed on an inventory and related only to one another, a definite number of objects. If we wanted to explain a certain incident of our psychological life, we could not search beyond the fact which we had already perceived. Think that all psychology was limited to the logical explanation of our decisions. Think of the meagre causative material at its disposal. And imagine what psychology can become now that Freud opens up to it the great reservoir of immersed causes.

Moreover, Freud himself is conscious of the revolution that the mere proclamation of the definite reality of the unconscious can produce in the history of ideas, and he does not restrain a feeling of pride; he exclaims:

> By attributing such importance to the unconscious in psychology, we have aroused a most evil spirit of criticism against psychoanalysis. . . . However, a great disappointment will be inflicted upon human megalomania by the psychological research of our time which proposes to show the *I* that it is not even master in its own house, that it is reduced to being satisfied with infrequent and fragmentary information about what goes on in its psychological life outside its consciousness. Psychoanalysts are neither the first nor the only ones to have appealed to modesty and meditation, but it appears that to them has fallen the mission of defending this way of seeing with the most ardour and of finding supporting evidence borrowed from experience and accessible to all.[3]

Let us reflect. Let us maintain, against our own belief so to speak, this principle of the unconscious as the seat of definite tendencies which rise up to modify the conscious; let us confront our experience with it. In other words, *let us think of all that we want without knowing that we do.*

Is not our life the constant search for goods, pleasures, satisfactions, that we do not dare admit we desire, that we do not even know we desire and seek? Is it not almost always *a posteriori* and only when we accomplish an act that we realise the long psychological work and the whole chain of latent feelings that led us towards it?

And furthermore, at what moment does the direct inspection of our consciousness give us exact information about all that we experience and all of which we are capable? Are we not always in constant ignorance of the degree and even of the existence of our feelings? Even in passion are there not moments when there seems to remain absolutely nothing of the passion, when it seems to be a pure construction of our minds? And yet, does it not continue to exist in an infinitely precise way, since the slightest accident which happens to encumber its course or to postpone its satisfaction can instantly provoke a complete upset in our whole being, an upset which is apparent even in our physical attitude, which affects even the circulation of our blood?

In love, for instance, is not a sincere lover constantly forced to resort to experiments and almost tricks to sound his feeling so as to know if it still exists? And this takes place at that very moment when, if someone came and told him that he must abandon hope or that he had been deceived, he would perhaps find himself very close to a crime.

So a first great discovery – it can perhaps be spoken of as a negative one, but negative discoveries are no less important than others – must be chalked up to the credit of Freud: the discovery that a great part of our psychological life takes place, so to speak, outside ourselves and can be disclosed and known only by a patient and complicated work based upon inference. In other words, we are never completely available to our minds, never completely conscious subjects.

The spirit in which I approach the study of Freud and the manner in which I intend to continue it must be clear in this first analysis. I do not intend to follow step by step all the developments of his thought. I simply search and seize one after another, without worrying about how they are linked, the points in his theory that seem to me to be capable of being expanded into psychological truths of general interest.

F.—2*

I am a desecrator who selfishly pillages a treasure and carries it off far from the temple. I may be judged severely from the moral point of view, but, in any case, must not be thought obliged to follow the slow, processional pace proper to the priests of Psychoanalysis.

Be willing now to leap with me to the examination of another Freudian idea that seems to me of considerable importance. I mean the idea of repression, to which must be attached censorship in dreams.

The essential part of it is known. From his experience as a practitioner, Freud thinks he can ascertain in every subject who is analysed, or simply questioned, an instinctive resistance to all questions, to every effort to penetrate the depths of his thought. Moreover, this resistance is subject to varying degrees of intensity. The patient is more or less hostile, more or less critical in accordance with the degree of unpleasantness of what the doctor is trying to bring to light.

Resistance, then, seems to be the result of a force of a properly affective nature, a force that is opposed to having certain psychological elements, which it considers incongruous and impossible to face directly, appear in full consciousness and be brought to light.

This force, encountered when one wants to work towards the cure of the patient, is that very one which first produced the illness by repressing a psychological process that was rising from the unconscious towards the conscious. In order to rise up a little further in spite of all, the repressed tendency transformed itself, disguised itself in fact as a mechanical act without apparent meaning. But it imposed itself invincibly upon the patient; it is the symptom. 'The symptom comes and is substituted for what has not been achieved.'[4]

Freud brings to light, then, the presence of an activity in consciousness which reduces or deforms our hidden spontaneity. He shows it at work in our dreams also and there calls it *the censor*. Just as during the war the censor either mutilated newspaper articles or forced their authors to present their thought in an approximate or veiled form only, so does a secret force modify and disguise our unconscious thoughts and allow them to approach our conscious mind only in the enigmatic form of a dream:

> The tendencies exercising censorship are those which the dreamer, in the judgement of his waking state recognizes as his, with which he feels in agreement. . . . The tendencies against which the censorship of dreams is directed . . . are those considered reprehensible or indecent from the point of view

of ethics, aesthetics, or society . . . are things we dare not think of, or which we think of only with horror ![5]

. . . [The neurotic symptoms] are the result of compromise, resulting from the interference of two opposing tendencies, and they express what has been repressed as well as what was the cause of the repression. The substitution may favour one of these tendencies more than the other, but rarely does it favour exclusively a single one.[6]

The dream likewise is a sort of composite, or rather it is a compromise among the repressed tendencies which gain force in sleep, and the tendencies that represent the true self and that continue to act by means of the deforming censor.

In other words, neurotic symptoms and dreams correspond to the efforts of our diverse 'sincerities' to appear at the same time.

The totality of this concept seems to me to be of an extraordinary importance and originality. Perhaps Freud himself did not perceive all the possibilities of generalisation which lie in it.

The discovery of a deceiving principle, a lying activity within us, can furnish an absolutely new view of all conscious life.

I am immediately going to exaggerate my idea: all our feelings are dreams; all our opinions are the exact equivalent of neurotic symptoms.

In us there is a constant, obstinate, ever-inventive tendency that urges us to camouflage ourselves in our own eyes. At any cost, we want ourselves to be and we construct ourselves other than we are in all situations. Naturally the direction of the deformation and its degree vary greatly in different natures, but, in all, the same principle of ruse and embellishment is at work.

To set out upon the study of the human heart without being informed of the existence and the activity of this principle and without preparing oneself against its subterfuges, is like wanting to determine the nature of the depths of the sea without a sounding instrument, by trusting the surface of the water alone. Or to quote Jules Romains who says it better, it is like making the traditional analysis which, 'even when it seeks the depths, allows itself to be guided by the visible surface indications. It does not suspect a deposit of iron unless the rocks above are all rusty, or of coal unless one treads upon black dust'.

Which of us is not acquainted with this demon that Freud calls the censor, this demon that constantly and subtly takes charge of our 'moral grooming'? At every moment, our whole being, I mean the confused, swarming mass of our appetites, is taken in hand and groomed by it. Into our lowest instincts it slips just that right amount of nobleness that will keep us from recognising them. It furnishes us abundantly with the pretexts, the colours we need in order to cover those little ignominious deeds we must commit so that we may live. It provides us with what we call our 'good reasons'. It keeps us in a state of friendliness and alliance with ourselves, a state without which we cannot live and yet a state so completely unjustified that we do not understand how it can exist.

But I feel that I am getting far from Freud's idea. The principle that presides over repression and censorship is far from working towards the triumph of our appetites. In Freud's thought, it fights them, stops them. Far from helping us to get around social conventions, it is both their representative and that of moral ideas.

There are cases where it is conquered, partially at least. The neurotic symptom, the dream, the slip, correspond to the relative success of the lower part of ourselves over it. And though it is not directly the agent of hypocrisy, it becomes so to the extent that it does not triumph.

When I claim that all our feelings, all our opinions, are dreams or obsessional acts, I mean that they are impure, masked, hypocritical states; I mean something that must be faced squarely: the fact that hypocrisy is inherent in consciousness.

Carrying Freud's idea to its conclusion, I shall say that to be conscious is to be hypocritical. Feelings, desires, come into consciousness only by breaking through a resistance whose imprint they keep, a resistance by which they are deformed. They become conscious only on condition that they do not appear to be what they are.

From this point of view, the chapter that Freud devotes to the methods used by the censor to deform and make unrecognisable the latent contents of the dream is worthy of reciving considerable extension. Several of these methods are certainly utilised by us in a waking state to help us depict our feelings to ourselves in an acceptable form. I mention only one as an example: the displacing or transfer of emphasis to one aspect, one aspect which is not the *essential*, of what we feel – or need to feel in order to be at peace; in other words, the rupture by the imagination of the centre of gravity of our complexes of feelings.

Let me say in passing that if at the beginning I appeared severe

towards the Freudian theory of the dream, it was largely because I was
sorry to see Freud apply too minutely to a special phenomenon an
idea that seemed to me to have infinite implications. His analysis of the
symbolism of dreams goes much too far; it reintroduces into consciousness, whose suppleness and extreme convertibility he has shown us,
something rigid that in my opinion should not be there. To understand
the full value of Freud's thought, one must retain if not vagueness, at
least a certain generality.

Before leaving this idea of the censor, we must grasp one other
aspect of it, an aspect that is of considerable importance.

When I say that hypocrisy is inherent in consciousness, I say too
much and too little. Censorship, the force that presides over repression,
is in part created from outside contributions, principally contributions
from education, that represent the influence of Society on the individual. All the same, these contributions are not entirely adventitious
or false. In the end they form a whole with the *I*. Freud even pictures
them as constitutive tendencies of the self.

And, in fact, it would be simplifying things a great deal to depict
only our inferior instincts as the truly constitutive parts of our personality. What represses them is also a part of ourselves.

But then a conclusion is evident: as ethical people, and even simply
as people, we are condemned to hypocrisy. Let us no longer call it
hypocrisy if you will. But we cannot avoid another word: impurity.
To live, to act, if we are to go methodically in a single direction, if we
are to trace our image on the retina of another, is to be composite,
impure, is to be a compromise.

Sincere comes from a Latin word meaning *pure* when speaking of
wine. It can be said that in integrity there is no sincerity for man. He
becomes sincere only if he dis-composes himself. Sincerity is then the
exact opposite to life. We must choose between the two.

The third point in Freud's theory that I think can be extended,
though not so far as the others, is his theory of sex.

You recall its general lines.

Freud, as we know, meditating upon the nature of the tendencies
that repression stops, which are expressed by the *substitution* of symptoms and dreams, thought that he could declare them all to be of a
sexual nature.

Several nuances must be noted at this point. Freud does not say, and even defends himself against the accusation of having said, that everything that appears in our dreams is of a sexual origin. Only what appears camouflaged is of sexual origin.

Moreover, Freud did not say, and defends himself again (for example, in the letter which Professor Claparède published as an appendix to the pamphlet *La Psychanalyse*), that our whole being is reduced to sexual tendencies or even that the *sexual instinct is the fundamental driving power of all the manifestations of psychological activity*. On the contrary:

> Psychoanalysis has never forgotten that non-sexual tendencies exist, and it has raised its edifice upon the principle of the clear and distinct separation of sexual tendencies from those referring to the ego; it has maintained, without waiting for objections, that the neuroses are the product not of sexuality, but of the conflict between the ego and sexuality.[7]

However it remains certain that the totality of spontaneous and unconscious tendencies in the depths of the individual seem to him to be identical with the sexual instinct.

Moreover, he is careful to define this instinct in a very broad way and to distinguish it from the instinct for procreation, even from purely genital activity. To stress its general character, he calls it *libido*.

The concept of *libido* is evidently not absolutely clear. At times it takes on an almost metaphysical value only to mean, a moment later, merely sexual appetite, properly called desire.

But I wonder if, instead of blaming Freud for his ambiguity, instead of wanting to force him to attach to this word *libido* an absolutely particular and limited tendency, it would not be better, on the contrary, to be grateful to him for his vagueness and for the leeway he allows. In the field with which we are concerned, I wonder if his main discovery is not precisely that of a single transformable tendency that may form the whole basis of our spontaneous psychological life.

In other words, the idea that desire is the driving force of all our activity, at least of our entire expansive activity – or better still, the idea that we are creators, productive beings, only in so far as we follow along in the direction of desire – seems to me to be admirably true and original.

But we must be careful not to betray by too much haste the very idea of Freud, and his concept of sublimation. So I continue.

By a long analysis, strongly backed with experimental observations, which fills the entire short pamphlet called *Three Essays on the Theory of Sex*, Freud establishes the fact that the sexual instinct has at first neither the object nor the aim that we assign to it. He shows that at first it is immanent, so to speak, throughout the being of the child, neither seeking nor suspecting any exterior satisfaction. This is the period he calls auto-erotic.

At the same time he shows the sexual instinct spreading invisibly and impartially to all organs and receiving satisfaction from any of them.

Then experience, which can, moreover, be preceded by outside interventions, teaches the *libido* to exteriorise itself. But even after this leap, it remains hesitant among several possible satisfactions and serves the genital act exclusively only at the onset of puberty, by a kind of synthetic, very complex operation, subject to a number of accidents.

This concept of desire as both beneath its object and exceeding or even transcending it is magnificent in audacity and depth.

We see all that Freud can explain by it. If the *libido* is repressed, one of two things happens: either it will return, in a form of satisfaction Freud calls pregenital, and cause a perversion through fixation, or it will produce an uneasiness that will give birth to neurosis.

But the very fact that it is not constitutionally linked to the genital act will allow it, on the other hand, to go beyond the act and to put itself into the service of the intellect; it will flood, so to speak, our mental faculties. Sublimation will consist in tapping the *libido* for the benefit of the intellect or even of morality.

The reflections inspired by this part of Freudian theory could be presented thus:

1. From the point of view of the psychology of creation, it is of considerable importance to have determined what we shall call the carnal sources of all the creations of the mind. This is of importance not in order to disparage the latter, but to show the unity of our psychological life, to demonstrate that we have only one sort of energy at our disposal, and that our complete liberty is limited to directing the use of it.

This is of importance in explaining both our aesthetic emotion when we stand before a great work of art and the sensual element that is always present in a sincere work of art, whatever may be the object represented.

It is even of importance from the point of view of aesthetic criticism, because it teaches us to seek in a work of art something more than that little repressed story which those who have applied psychoanalysis to art up to the present time have pursued with, in my opinion, too much precision. It teaches us to see the current of desire, the enthusiasm from which the work was born. A sort of aesthetic criterion should be set up to distinguish between works born of an inclination and those fabricated at will – the aesthetic quality not being taken into consideration.

2. By analysing first what the *libido* constructs in the unconscious under the shelter of repression, and then all that the repression of the *libido* can produce in conscious life, Freud opens up a tremendous realm to psychology.

I do not think that the analysis of dreams, practised in accordance with Freudian orthodoxy can lead to very much of interest, especially because of the strange, previously established telegraphic code that imprisons interpretation.

But think what a psychologist without either Freudian or anti-Freudian prejudice can discover if he has simply decided not to be unaware of what I should like to call the sexual state of the human beings he is studying. Think of those depths, as yet so poorly explored, of sexual attractions and especially, perhaps, of sexual hatreds. Think how the knowledge of the sexual experiences of a certain human being, and especially of the repercussions created by these experiences, could give access to an individual character, could give a key to a whole behaviour.

Up to the present, a novelist has been careful to visualise to himself the social situation, the conditions of existence, the profession, the ancestors, of each of his heroes, although he may not have noted these down. After Freud, it seems impossible to me that he can fail to imagine ahead of time in the same way, though he may say nothing about it in the course of his story (the aim of his story may even be merely to suggest it), the sexual situation of each one of his heroes and his sexual relation to others. You understand that I give the word its most general meaning.

3. By detaching the *libido* from its object, Freud takes sides implicitly with the subjectivist conception of love. It is evident that this mobile,

shifting desire he describes will not have to receive anything from its chosen object, will not even be able to receive anything, and that the mind of the lover will form from the image of the beloved object from its own resources alone.

Somewhere he speaks of the *overevaluation of the sexual object*. He probably means this primarily in the physical sense, but he is certainly also thinking that all the moral beauties with which the lover adorns the beloved are the reflection of the projection of the *libido* on the beloved. He admits then that all love is hallucinatory, seeking in outsiders only a pretext for settling down. He does not admit the appeal, the attraction, that one human being has for another, nor does he admit that love can ever be born from real and objective affinities.

Now we must try to encompass in a single glance the total of Freud's theory and attempt to evaluate it.

Freud brings us two things. He brings us a new world of facts, a new 'family' of facts (on this question I differ completely from Jules Romains, who argues against his having made this sort of discovery). And even if he has not given us a new 'law' among these facts, he has at least brought us a new method for exploring them or, more vaguely, a new attitude to take in respect to them.

The new world is that of the unconscious conceived of and demonstrated as a system of definite facts, for the first time having the same nature, made of the same material, as those which appear in consciousness, and having a constant relationship, being in constant exchange with conscious facts.

Freud reveals the lush flora of sexual tendencies and complexes among these unconscious facts. Though he describes them in too much detail (a common fault of his), though he standardises them too much, the mere fact of having revealed them is of admirable originality.

Others with a lighter touch and a keener sense of the individual will be able to follow him into this strange garden.

But he already has shown others what attitude must be adopted in order to make good observations (and this is his second, equally priceless, contribution). He makes us aware of the force at work within us, attempting to deceive us about ourselves; he teaches us its tricks, and the ways of outwitting them.

More generally, he sketches a new introspective attitude that can be the basis of a whole new orientation of psychological research. This attitude consists in attempting to know oneself through signs alone. Instead of listening to the feelings themselves or the sensations, Freud seeks them out in their results alone, in their symptoms.

Well before his time, people had certainly tried to grasp psychological phenomena indirectly in order to attain more certainty, especially when it was a question of social condition. All psychophysiology was an effort to acquire information about the conscious, starting from the exterior, from something that was not it but that had in its favour the fact that it could be touched, measured, made to vary. But psychotherapy made the error, which Bergson pointed out, of disregarding the differences in the quality of the phenomena.

In turn, Bergson's error, which I point out only in the most prudent and hypothetical manner, was perhaps to plunge with too great confidence into the pure psychological flood and, with too much naïveté, to expect knowledge from the single ebb that he had known. Can the course of a river be plotted by swimming in it?

Freud avoids the error of the psychophysiologists by accepting psychological facts alone as information on psychological life. He constructs an independent, autonomous psychology. This is one of the reasons for the resistance that he has encountered.

On the other hand, he does not believe these psychological facts; I mean that he does not accept them at face value. He looks at them *a priori* as being lies, which are, however, capable of being explained. He uses them as signs in order to go back through induction to the deepest and most masked psychological reality. He pushes backwards against the vital flow.

And so he gives back to intelligence that active role, that role of distrust and penetration that has always been the only one that allows and favours knowledge in all categories. There would be much to say about his complete faith in psychological determinism. But as a method that must be used as long as possible, determinism is unassailable. Only by siding with it can we hope to reach into that chaos which our inner self sends out to greet us, and to gain some clarity and profit for thought.

SOURCE: Jacques Rivière, *The Ideal Reader* (1960).

NOTES

1. *Introduction a la psychanalyse*, Part III, ch. 18, p. 288 [of the French translation. Since Rivière read the French translation of Freud's work and drew his conclusions from the French text, it seemed valid to translate the French text instead of inserting quotations from the standard English translation, which Rivière naturally did not know.].

2. Ibid. p. 289.

3. Ibid. p. 296.

4. Ibid. Part III, ch. 19, p. 305.

5. Ibid. Part II, ch. 9, p. 145.

6. Ibid. Part III, ch. 19, p. 313.

7. Ibid. Part III, ch. 22, p. 365.

GEORGE SANTAYANA

A Long Way Round to Nirvana (1923)

Development of a Suggestion found in Freud's *Beyond the Pleasure Principle*

THAT the end of life is death may be called a truism, since the various kinds of immortality that might perhaps supervene would none of them abolish death, but at best would weave life and death together into the texture of a more comprehensive destiny. The end of one life might be the beginning of another, if the Creator had composed his great work like a dramatic poet, assigning successive lines to different characters. Death would then be merely the cue at the end of each speech, summoning the next personage to break in and keep the ball rolling. Or perhaps, as some suppose, all the characters are assumed in turn by a single supernatural Spirit, who amid his endless improvisations is imagining himself living for the moment in this particular solar and social system. Death in such a universal monologue would be but a change of scene or of metre, while in the scramble of a real comedy it would be a change of actors. In either case every voice would be silenced sooner or later, and death would end each particular life, in spite of all possible sequels.

The relapse of created things into nothing is no violent fatality, but something naturally quite smooth and proper. This has been set forth recently, in a novel way, by a philosopher from whom we hardly expected such a lesson, namely Professor Sigmund Freud. He has now broadened his conception of sexual craving or *libido* into a general principle of attraction or concretion in matter, like the Eros of the ancient poets Hesiod and Empedocles. The windows of that stuffy clinic have been thrown open; that smell of acrid disinfectants, those hysterical shrieks, have escaped into the cold night. The troubles of the sick soul, we are given to understand, as well as their cure, after all flow from the stars.

I am glad that Freud has resisted the tendency to represent this principle of Love as the only principle in nature. Unity somehow exercises an evil spell over metaphysicians. It is admitted that in real life it is not well for One to be alone, and I think pure unity is no less barren and graceless in metaphysics. You must have plurality to start with, or trinity, or at least duality, if you wish to get anywhere, even if you wish to get effectively into the bosom of the One, abandoning your separate existence. Freud, like Empedocles, has prudently introduced a prior principle for Love to play with; not Strife, however (which is only an incident in Love), but Inertia, or the tendency towards peace and death. Let us suppose that matter was originally dead, and perfectly content to be so, and that it still relapses, when it can, into its old equilibrium. But the homogeneous (as Spencer would say) when it is finite is unstable: and matter, presumably not being co-extensive with space, necessarily forms aggregates which have an inside and an outside. The parts of such bodies are accordingly differently exposed to external influences and differently related to one another. This inequality, even in what seems most quiescent, is big with changes, destined to produce in time a wonderful complexity. It is the source of all uneasiness, of life, and of love.

Let us imagine [writes Freud][1] an undifferentiated vesicle of sensitive substance: then its surface, exposed as it is to the outer world, is by its very position differentiated, and serves as an organ for receiving stimuli. . . . This morsel of living substance floats about in an outer world which is charged with the most potent energies, and it would be destroyed . . . if it were not furnished with protection against stimulation. [On the other hand] the sensitive cortical layer has no protective barrier against excitations emanating from within. . . . The most prolific sources of such excitations are the so-called instincts of the organism. . . . The child never gets tired of demanding the repetition of a game . . . he wants always to hear the same story instead of a new one, insists inexorably on exact repetition, and corrects each deviation which the narrator lets slip by mistake. . . . According to this, *an instinct would be a tendency in living organic matter impelling it towards reinstatement of an earlier condition*, one which it had abandoned under the influence of external disturbing forces – a kind of organic elasticity, or, to put it another way, the manifestation of inertia in organic life.

If, then, all organic instincts are conservative, historically acquired, and directed towards regression, towards reinstatement of something earlier, we are obliged to place all the results of organic development to the credit of external, disturbing, and distracting influences. The rudimentary creature would from its very beginning not have wanted to change, would, if circumstances had remained the same, have always merely repeated the same course of existence. . . . It would be counter to the conservative nature of instinct if the goal of life were a state never hitherto reached. It must be rather an ancient starting point, which the living being left long ago, and to which it harks back again by all the circuitous paths of development. . . . *The goal of all life is death.* . . .

Through a long period of time the living substance may have . . . had death within easy reach . . . until decisive external influences altered in such a way as to compel [it] to ever greater deviations from the original path of life, and to ever more complicated and circuitous routes to the attainment of the goal of death. These circuitous ways to death, faithfully retained by the conservative instincts, would be neither more nor less than the phenomena of life as we know it.

Freud puts forth these interesting suggestions with much modesty, admitting that they are vague and uncertain and (what it is even more important to notice) mythical in their terms; but it seems to me that, for all that, they are an admirable counterblast to prevalent follies. When we hear that there is, animating the whole universe, an *Elan vital*, or general impulse toward some unknown but single ideal, the terms used are no less uncertain, mythical, and vague, but the suggestion conveyed is false – false, I mean, to the organic source of life and aspiration, to the simple naturalness of nature: whereas the suggestion conveyed by Freud's speculations is true. In what sense can myths and metaphors be true or false? In the sense that, in terms drawn from moral predicaments or from literary psychology, they may report the general movement and the pertinent issue of material facts, and may inspire us with a wise sentiment in their presence. In this sense I should say that Greek mythology was true and Calvinist theology was false. The chief terms employed in psycho-analysis have always been metaphorical: 'unconscious wishes', 'the pleasure-principle', 'the Oedipus complex', 'Narcissism', 'the censor'; nevertheless, interesting and profound vistas may be opened up, in such terms, into the tangle of events in a man's life, and a fresh start may be made with fewer encumberances and less morbid inhibition. 'The shortcomings of our description', Freud says, 'would probably disappear if for psychological terms we could substitute physiological or chemical ones. These too only constitute a metaphorical language, but one familiar to us for a

much longer time, and perhaps also simpler.' All human discourse is
metaphorical, in that our perceptions and thoughts are adventitious
signs for their objects, as names are, and by no means copies of what is
going on materially in the depths of nature; but just as the sportsman's
eye, which yields but a summary graphic image, can trace the flight of
a bird through the air quite well enough to shoot it and bring it down,
so the myths of a wise philosopher about the origin of life or of dreams,
though expressed symbolically, may reveal the pertinent movement
of nature to us, and may kindle in us just sentiments and true expectations in respect to our fate – for his own soul is the bird this sportsman
is shooting.

Now I think these new myths of Freud's about life, like his old ones
about dreams, are calculated to enlighten and to chasten us enormously
about ourselves. The human spirit, when it awakes, finds itself in
trouble; it is burdened, for no reason it can assign, with all sorts of
anxieties about food, pressures, pricks, noises, and pains. It is born, as
another wise myth has it, in original sin. And the passions and ambitions
of life, as they come on, only complicate this burden and make it
heavier, without rendering it less incessant or gratuitous. Whence this
fatality, and whither does it lead; It comes from heredity, and it leads
to propagation. When we ask how heredity could be started or trans-
mitted, our ignorance of nature and of past time reduces us to silence
or to wild conjectures. Something – let us call it matter – must always
have existed, and some of its parts, under pressure of the others, must
have got tied up into knots, like the mainspring of a watch, in such a
violent and unhappy manner that when the pressure is relaxed they
fly open as fast as they can, and unravel themselves with a vast sense
of relief. Hence the longing to satisfy latent passions, with the fugitive
pleasure in doing so. But the external agencies that originally wound
up that mainspring never cease to operate; every fresh stimulus gives
it another turn, until it snaps, or grows flaccid, or is unhinged. Moreover, from time to time, when circumstances change, these external
agencies may encrust that primary organ with minor organs attached
to it. Every impression, every adventure, leaves a trace or rather a
seed behind it. It produces a further complication in the structure of the
body, a fresh charge, which tends to repeat the impressed motion in
season and out of season. Hence that perpetual docility or ductility in
living substance which enables it to learn tricks, to remember facts, and

(when the seeds of past experiences marry and cross in the brain) to imagine new experiences, pleasing or horrible. Every act initiates a new habit and may implant a new instinct. We see people even late in life carried away by political or religious contagions or developing strange vices; there would be no peace in old age, but rather a greater and greater obsession by all sorts of cares, were it not that time, in exposing us to many adventitious influences, weakens or discharges our primitive passions; we are less greedy, less lusty, less hopeful, less generous. But these weakened primitive impulses are naturally by far the strongest and most deeply rooted in the organism: so that although an old man may be converted or may take up some hobby, there is usually something thin in his elderly zeal, compared with the heartiness of youth; nor is it edifying to see a soul in which the plainer human passions are extinct becoming a hotbed of chance delusions.

In any case each fresh habit taking root in the organism forms a little mainspring or instinct of its own, like a parasite; so that an elaborate mechanism is gradually developed, where each lever and spring holds the other down, and all hold the mainspring down together, allowing it to unwind itself only very gradually, and meantime keeping the whole clock ticking and revolving, and causing the smooth outer face which it turns to the world, so clean and innocent, to mark the time of day amiably for the passer-by. But there is a terribly complicated labour going on beneath, propelled with difficulty, and balanced precariously, with much secret friction and failure. No wonder that the engine often gets visibly out of order, or stops short: the marvel is that it ever manages to go at all. Nor is it satisfied with simply revolving and, when at last dismounted, starting afresh in the person of some seed it has dropped, a portion of its substance with all its concentrated instincts wound up tightly within it, and eager to repeat the ancestral experiment; all this growth is not merely material and vain. Each clock in revolving strikes the hour, even the quarters, and often with lovely chimes. These chimes we call perceptions, feelings, purposes, and dreams; and it is because we are taken up entirely with this mental music, and perhaps think that it sounds of itself and needs no music-box to make it, that we find such difficulty in conceiving the nature of our own clocks and are compelled to describe them only musically, that is, in myths. But the ineptitude of our aesthetic minds to unravel the nature of mechanism does not deprive these minds of their own clearness and euphony. Besides sounding their various musical notes, they have the cognitive function of indicating the hour and catching the echoes of distant events or of maturing inward dispositions. This information and emotion, added to incidental pleasures in satisfying our various passions, make up the life of an incarnate spirit. They reconcile it to the external fatality that has wound up the organism, and is breaking it down; and they rescue this organism and all its works from the indignity of being a vain complication and a waste of motion.

That the end of life should be death may sound sad: yet what other end can anything have? The end of an evening party is to go to bed; but its use is to gather congenial people together, that they may pass the time pleasantly. An invitation to the dance is not rendered ironical because the dance cannot last for ever; the youngest of us and the most vigorously wound up, after a few hours, has had enough of sinuous stepping and prancing. The transitoriness of things is essential to their physical being, and not at all sad in itself; it becomes sad by virtue of a sentimental illusion, which makes us imagine that they wish to endure and that their end is always untimely; but in a healthy nature it is not, so. What is truly sad is to have some impulse frustrated in the midst of its career, and robbed of its chosen object; and what is painful is to have an organ lacerated or destroyed when it is still vigorous, and not ready for its natural sleep and dissolution. We must not confuse the itch which our unsatisfied instincts continue to cause with the pleasure of satisfying and dismissing each of them in turn. Could they all be satisfied harmoniously we should be satisfied once for all and completely. Then doing and dying would coincide throughout and be a perfect pleasure.

This same insight is contained in another wise myth which has inspired morality and religion in India from time immemorial: I mean the doctrine of Karma. We are born, it says, with a heritage, a character imposed, and a long task assigned, all due to the ignorance which in our past lives has led us into all sorts of commitments. These obligations we must pay off, relieving the pure spirit within us from its accumulated burdens, from debts and assets both equally oppressive. We cannot disentangle ourselves by mere frivolity, nor by suicide: frivolity would only involve us more deeply in the toils of fate, and suicide would but truncate our misery and leave us for ever a confessed failure. When life is understood to be a process of redemption, its various phases are taken up in turn without haste and without undue attachment; their coming and going have all the keenness of pleasure, the holiness of sacrifice, and the beauty of art. The point is to have expressed and discharged all that was latent in us; and to this perfect relief various temperaments and various traditions assign different names, calling it having one's day, or doing one's duty, or realising one's ideal, or saving one's soul. The task in any case is definite and imposed on us by nature, whether we recognise it or not; therefore we can make true moral progress or fall into real errors. Wisdom and genius lie in discerning this prescribed task and in doing it readily, cleanly, and without distraction. Folly on the contrary imagines that any scent is worth following, that we have an infinite nature, or no nature in particular, that life begins without obligations and can do business without capital, and that the will is vacuously free, instead of being a specific burden and a tight hereditary knot to be unravelled. Some philosophers without self-knowledge think that the variations and further entanglements which the future may bring are the manifestation of spirit; but they are, as Freud has indicated, imposed on living beings by external pressure, and take shape in the realm of matter. It is only after the organs of spirit are formed mechanically that spirit can exist, and can distinguish the better from the worse in the fate of those organs, and therefore in its own fate. Spirit has nothing to do with infinite existence. Infinite existence is something physical and ambiguous; there is no scale in it and no centre. The depths of the human heart are finite, and they are dark only to ignorance. Deep and dark as a soul may be when you look down into it from outside, it is something perfectly natural; and the same understanding that can unearth our suppressed young passions, and dispel our stubborn bad habits, can show us where our true good lies. Nature has marked out the path for us beforehand; there are snares in it, but also primroses, and it leads to peace.

SOURCE: George Santayana, *Some Turns of Thought in Modern Philosophy* (1933).

NOTES

1. The following quotations are drawn from *Beyond the Pleasure Principle*, by Sigmund Freud, authorised translation by C. J. M. Hubback (The International Psycho-Analytic Press, 1922) pp. 29–48. The italics are in the original.

C. G. JUNG

Sigmund Freud in His Historical Setting (1933)

IT is always a delicate and dangerous task to try to give a living man his historical value. But at least it is far more possible to grasp any man's significance and the extent to which he has been conditioned by history, if his life-work and system of thought lie completed before us as do Freud's. His teaching, which in its fundamental features is probably known to every educated layman today, is not limitless in its ramifications, nor does it include any alien component, the origin of which lies in other fields of science; it is based on a few transparent principles, which, to the exclusion of everything else, dominate and permeate all the material of his thought. The originator of this teaching has also identified it with his method of 'psychoanalysis,' and in doing so has made a rigid system rightly charged with being absolute. But on the other hand, this coinage of a theory marked itself as something extraordinary in the history of science, has a great advantage in that it stands out in bold relief as a strange and unique phenomenon against its philosophical and scientific background. Nowhere does it merge with other contemporary concepts, nor has its author made any conscious effort to connect it with its historical ancestors. This quality of detachment is still more heightened by a peculiar terminology which at times borders on a subjective jargon. To all appearances – and Freud would prefer to have it that way – it is as if this teaching had developed exclusively in the doctor's consulting room, and was unwelcome to everyone but himself, and a thorn in the flesh of academic 'science'. And yet, even the most original and detached idea does not fall from heaven, but grows out of an objective root-system in which all contemporaries are closely united whether they recognise it or not.

The historical conditions which preceded Freud and formed his groundwork made a phenomenon like himself necessary, and it is precisely his main thesis, that is, the doctrine of the *repression of sexuality*, which is most clearly conditioned in this historical sense. Freud stands like his greater, philosophical, contemporary, Nietzsche, at the end of the Victorian era which, on the continent, never received such an appropriate epithet, despite the fact that it was just as characteristic in Germanic and Protestant countries generally, as among Anglo-Saxons. The Victorian era was a period of repression, a convulsive attempt to keep artificially alive by moralisings, anaemic ideals framed in a bourgeois respectability. These 'ideals', the last off-shoots of the collective religious ideas of the Middle Ages, shortly before the Victorian epoch had been severely damaged by the French period of enlightenment and the consequent revolution. Hand in hand with this, ancient truths in the political field had become hollow and threatened to collapse. However, it was still a little too soon for the final over-throw, and consequently the whole nineteenth century strove franti-cally to keep alive the disappearing Christian Middle Ages. Political revolutions were stamped out, efforts toward moral freedom were thwarted by bourgeois public opinion, and the critical philosophy of the out-going eighteenth century at first emptied itself into renewed, systematic attempts to capture the world in a single network of thought in a way similar to what had been done in medieval times. But in the course of the nineteenth century enlightenment slowly broke through, especially in the form of scientific materialism and rationalism. This is the matrix out of which Freud grew, and it is the mental characteristics of this matrix which have shaped him along foreordained lines. He has a passion for bringing everything under the light of reason exactly as in the eighteenth century – one of his favourite citations is Voltaire's '*Ecrasez l'infame*'; with a certain satisfaction he invariably points out the flaw in the crystal; all complex psychic phenomena like art, phil-osophy, and religion fall under his suspicion, and appear as 'nothing but' repressions of the sexual instinct. As we have noted, this essentially reductive and negative attitude towards recognised cultural values rests in Freud's case on the historical conditions which immediately preceded him. He sees as his time forces him to see. This comes most clearly to light in his essay, 'The Future of an Illusion', where he draws a picture of religion which corresponds completely with the prejudices of the materialistic age.

His revolutionary tendency to find always the negative explanation for things is based on the historical fact that the Victorian epoch has fraudulently used cultural values in such a way as to produce a middle-class idea of the world, and among the means employed, religion (more correctly a repression-religion), played the chief part. It is this sham idea of religion that hovers before Freud's eyes. The same is true of his idea of man. Man's conscious qualities – all Victorian – his idealistic, counterfeited personality, rest on corresponding dark back-grounds, that is, repressed infantile sexuality; every positive gift depends on an infantile minus quantity as suggested in the materialistic *bon mot*: '*Der mensch ist was er isst*.' (Man is what he eats.)

This conception of man, considered historically, is a reaction to the tendency of the Victorian era to *see* everything in a 'rosy' light, and to *describe* everything *sub rosa*, for it was the time of mental 'pussyfooting', which finally brought to birth a Nietzsche who used a hammer in his philosophising. Consequently, ethical motives as final and indisputable factors in human life, disappear in the Freudian teaching. They are supplanted by a conventional morality about which it is rightly as-sumed that it would never have existed in this form, or never have existed at all, if one or more bad-tempered ancestors had not invented such precepts as a protection against the evil consequences of their impotence. These concepts, it is further assumed, have (unfortunately) been in existence since then, and continue in the 'super-ego' of every individual. This grotesque, depreciative concept is a just punishment for the historical fact that the ethics of the Victorian era were merely a conventional morality, the creation of bileous *praeceptores mundi*.

If Freud is viewed in this retrospective way, that is, as an exponent of the *ressentiment* of the incoming century against the nineteenth, with its illusions, its hypocrisy, its half-ignorance, its false, overwrought feelings, its shallow morality, its artificial, sapless religiosity, and its lamentable taste, he can be viewed in my opinion much more correctly than when the attempt is made to mark him out as the herald of new ways and new truths. He is a great destroyer who breaks the chains of the past. He liberates us from the unhealthy pressure of an ancient world of rotten habits. He shows how the values in which our parents still believe may be understood in an altogether different sense: for example, such a sentimental fraud as that of parents 'who live only for their children'; or the theme of the noble son who 'is at his mother's feet all his life'; or the ideal of the daughter who has a 'perfect under-standing of her father'. Previously these things were believed uncriti-

cally, but since Freud has brought into the forum as an object of discussion the unsavoury idea of the incestuous fixation, there have been
aroused useful doubts – for reasons of good health, be it noted, they
must not go too far!

The 'sexual theory', to be correctly understood, should be taken as a
negative critique of our contemporary psychology. We can become
reconciled even to its most disturbing views and assertions if we know
against what historical conditions they are directed. If we know how
the nineteenth century twisted quite natural things into sentimental,
moralistic virtues in order not to have its picture of the world disturbed, then we can also understand something of the meaning of the
Freudian assertion that the suckling already experiences sexuality at its
mother's breast, an assertion which, above all others, has aroused the
greatest commotion. This interpretation cast suspicion on the axiomatic innocence of the child at the breast, that is, the mother-child
relationship. This is the essential thing about the assertion – it is a shot
aimed at the heart of 'holy motherhood'. That mothers carry children
is not holy, but natural. Should it be said to be holy, then a strong suspicion is aroused that something very unholy has to be covered up by
it. Freud has said out loud 'what is behind it' – only he has unfortunately
blackened the suckling instead of the mother.

Scientifically, the theory of the sexuality of the suckling has little
value. It is a matter of indifference to the caterpillar whether we say of
it that it eats its leaf with ordinary pleasure or with sexual pleasure.
Freud's world-historical contribution does not consist in these scholastic
mistakes of interpretation in the special scientific field, but in the fact
on which his fame is founded and justified, namely, that, like an Old
Testament Prophet, he overthrew false idols and pitilessly spread out
to view the rottenness of the contemporary soul. Wherever he applies
a painful reduction (for example, in explaining our God of the nineteenth century as a glorification of 'Papa', or the hoardings of money as
an infantile pleasure in excrement, etc.), we can be sure that a collective
overvaluation or falsification is called into question. Where, for instance, in the annals of Victorianism is the sentimental God of the
nineteenth century ever faced with a *deus absconditus* as in Luther's
teaching? Is it not assumed, to mention yet another Victorian belief,
that all good people also earn much money?

Like Nietzsche, like the Great War, so too Freud (and his literary

replica, *Joyce*), is an answer to the sickness of the nineteenth century.
That is certainly his chief significance. Looking forward, he offers no
constructive plan, because not even the boldest effort or the strongest
will would ever be able to live out freely all the repressed incest wishes
and other incompatibilities to be met with in the psyche. Far from this,
Protestant ministers have already plunged into psychoanalysis and applied it in a distinctly reactionary way. It seems to them an excellent
means of sensitising the consciences of people to yet more sins than
merely conscious ones – a truly grotesque, but extremely logical turn
of events prophesied years ago by Stanley Hall (see his *Autobiography*).
Even the Freudian physicians are beginning to confess to a new, and if
possible, even more soulless repression, something quite understandable
too, because no one knows what to do with the incompatible wishes.
On the contrary, one begins again to understand the necessity of repression.

As a relief for this distress of conscience, Freud has invented the idea
of *sublimation*. The idea of sublimation means nothing less than the
trick of the alchemist, the transformation of the base into the noble, the
bad into the good, the useless into the useful. Whoever could accomplish this would certainly have earned immortal fame. Unfortunately,
the reconversion of energy without the consumption of a still greater
quantity of energy applied to this purpose has never yet been discovered by the physicists. 'Sublimation' is, for the present, a pious
wish-structure invented for the quieting of inopportune questioners.

In discussing these problems, however, I do not wish to put the
chief emphasis on the professional difficulty of practical psychotherapy
but rather on the evident fact that Freud's theory does not stand for a
new way of life, a guiding line of development. He is not to be understood from a forward-looking view; everything in him is oriented
backwards, and this too, with a one-sided bias. His only interest is
where things come from, never where they are going. It is more than
a scientific, causal need that drives him to seek for causes, since otherwise it could not have escaped him that certain psychological facts
have explanations entirely different from those based on the ineptitudes
of the *chronique scandaleuse*.

An excellent example of this is the essay on Leonardo da Vinci and
his problem of the two mothers. As a matter of fact, Leonardo did
have an illegitimate mother and a step-mother, but in reality the dual

mother problem may always be present as a mythological motif, even
when the two real mothers do not exist. Heroes very often have two
mothers, and for the Pharaohs this mythological custom was actually
de rigeur. But Freud stops at the unfavourable fact; he contents himself
with the idea that *naturally* something disagreeable or negative lies
concealed in the situation. Although this procedure is not exactly
'scientific', yet, considered historically, I credit it with a still greater
merit than if it were scientifically impeccable. One-sided though his
explanation is, it is important for the time. All too easily the dark
backgrounds that are present in this problem of Leonardo's could be
obliterated by scientific accuracy, and then Freud's world-historical
task of showing up the darkness behind the false façades would not be
fulfilled. A small scientific inexactitude has little meaning in this
connection. If we go through his works carefully and critically, we
really have the impression that his scientific capability and its goal,
which Freud pushes into the foreground again and again, has been
secretly diverted to the uses of the cultural task of which he himself is
unconscious, and that this has happened at the expense of the development of his theory. Today, the voice of one calling in the wilderness
must perforce ring out with scientific tones if the ear of the contemporary world is to be reached. At all costs we must say that it is science
which has brought such facts to the light of day, regardless of whether
science has done it or not. That alone is really convincing. But even
science is not proof against the unconscious *Weltanschauung*. How easy
it would have been to take Leonardo's Anna with the Virgin and Christ
as the classical representation of the mythological motif of the dual
mothers. But for Freud's late Victorian psychology, and for an infinitely large public as well, very much more has been gained if after
'thorough investigation' it developed that Leonardo's respectable
father caused the existence of the great artist by reason of a small
indiscretion! This thrust strikes home, and Freud makes the thrust not
because he consciously wants to abandon science for gossip, but because he is under compulsion from the *Zeitgeist* to expose the possible
dark sides of the human soul. The mythological motif of the two
mothers is the really scientific clue to the enigma, but that only stirs
the few to whom the truth really matters however inopportune it may
be. The larger proportion of the public, however, is left cold by such a
hypothesis, because to them the one-sided, negatively disposed

explanation means much more than it does to science which is above programmatic truth.

As it is assumed, science strives for an impartial, unbiased, and in-clusive judgement. The Freudian theory, on the other hand, is at best a partial truth, and therefore in order to maintain itself and be effective, it has the rigidity of a dogma and the fanaticism of an inquisitor. For a scientific truth a simple statement suffices, but, at bottom, psychoanalytic theory prefers programmatic truth because it reaches a wider public. And in this can be recognised its origin in the doctor's consulting room. It preaches those things which are of paramount importance to the neurotic of the early twentieth century because he is one of the un-conscious victims of late Victorian psychology. Psychoanalysis destroys the false values in the neurotic personality by cauterising away the rottenness of the dead nineteenth century. Thus far, the method means a valuable, even an indispensable increase in practical knowledge which has advanced the study of the psychology of the neuroses in the most efficient way. We have to thank the bold one-sidedness of Freud if medicine is now in a position to handle cases of neurosis individually, and if science is enriched by a method which permits it to work with an individual psyche as an object of research. Before Freud, this only occurred as a curiosity.

But in so far as the neurosis is not a disease specific to the Victorian era, but enjoys a general distribution in time and space, and is therefore present among peoples or individuals who are not in need of any special sexual enlightment, nor open to any assumptions as to harmful sexual disturbances in their lives, a theory of neurosis or a theory of dreams based on a Victorian prejudice is at the most of very secondary import to science. If it were not so, Adler's entirely different conception would have fallen flat and had no effect. Adler reduces everything, not to pleasure, but to the power tendency, and the success of his theory is not to be denied. This fact brings out with dazzling clearness the one-sidedness, but, taken with the Freudian view, there has already resulted from it a more extensive and still clearer picture of the *ressentiment* against the spirit of the nineteenth century. All of the modern defection from the exploded ideals of our fathers is again mirrored in Adler.

But the human soul is not just a product of the *Zeitgeist*; it is a thing of far greater persistence and immutability. The 'nineteenth century' is a merely local and passing phenomenon, which has only deposited a relatively thin layer of dust on the age-old soul of mankind. But if this layer is wiped off, if our professional eye-glasses are once cleaned, what shall we see then? How shall we look upon the soul, and how shall we explain a neurosis? This problem presents itself to every practitioner whose cases are not cured even after all the childhood sexual experiences have been dug up, and all the cultural values dissected into bad elements, or when the patient has become that strange fiction – a normal man and a gregarious animal.

A general psychological theory which lays claim to being scientific must not found itself on the malformations of the nineteenth century, and a theory of neurosis must also be capable of explaining hysteria among the Maoris. As soon as the sexual theory leaves the field of the special psychology of neuroses and reaches out into other fields, as for example that of primitive psychology, its one-sidedness and inadequacy leap to the eye. Views which have developed out of the observation of Viennese neuroses between 1890 and 1920 prove themselves poor tools when applied to problems of totem and taboo, even when the application is made in a very clever way. Freud has not penetrated into that deeper layer of what is common to all humanity. He ought not to have done it, nor could he do it without being untrue to his cultural historical task. And this task he has fulfilled – a task enough to fill a whole life's work, and fully deserving the fame it has won.

SOURCE: *Journal of Personality* (1933), article translated by Cary F. Baynes; reprinted in G. Adler, M. Fordham, H. Kead (eds.), *The Collected Works of C. G. Jung* (1966).

THOMAS MANN

Freud and the Future (1936)

[A speech delivered in Vienna, 9 May 1936, on Freud's eightieth birthday]

WE are gathered here to do honour to a great scientist. And the question may very properly be raised: what justifies a man of letters in assuming the role of spokesman on such an occasion? Or, passing on the responsibility to the members of the learned society which chose him, why should they not have selected one of their own kind, a man of science, rather than an author, to celebrate in words the birthday of their master? For an author, my friends, is a man essentially not bent upon science, upon knowing, distinguishing, and analysing; he stands for simple creation, for doing and making, and thus may be the object of useful cognition, without, by his very nature, having any competence in it as subject. But is it, perhaps, that the author in his character as artist, and artist in the field of the intellect, is especially called to the celebration of feasts of the mind; that he is by nature more a man of feast-days than the scientist and man of knowledge? It is not for me to dispute such a view. It is true, the poet has understanding of the feasts of life, understanding even of life as a feast – and here I am just touching, very lightly for the moment, upon a theme that may become a main motif in the chorus of homage which we are to perform this evening. But it is more likely that the sponsors of this evening had something else in mind in their choice: that is to say, the solemn and novel confrontation of object and subject, the object of knowledge with the knower – a saturnalia, as it were, in which the knower and seer of dreams himself becomes, by our act of homage, the object of dreamlike penetration. And to such a position I could not object, either; particularly because it strikes a chord capable in the future of great symphonic development. It will recur, more clearly accented and fully instrumented. For, unless I am greatly mistaken, it is just this confrontation of object and subject, their mingling and identification, the resultant insight into the mysterious unity of ego and actuality, destiny and character, doing and happening, and thus into the mystery of reality as an operation of the psyche – it is just this confrontation that is the alpha and omega of all psychoanalytical knowledge.

Be that as it may, the choice of an artist as the encomiast of a great scientist is a comment upon both. In the first place, one deduces from it a connection between the man of genius we now honour and the world of creative literature; in the second place, it displays the peculiar relations between the writer and the field of science whose declared and acknowledged master and creator the other is. Now, the unique and remarkable thing about this mutual close relation is that it remained for so long unconscious – that is, in that region of the soul which we have learned to call the unconscious, a realm whose discovery and investigation, whose conquest for humanity, are precisely the task and mission of the wise genius whose fame we celebrate. The close relation between literature and psychoanalysis has been known for a long time to both sides. But the solemn significance of this hour lies, at least in my eyes and as a matter of personal feeling, in that on this evening there is taking place the first official meeting between the two spheres, in the acknowledgement and demonstration of their relationship.

I repeat that the profound sympathy between the two spheres had existed for a long time unperceived. Actually we know that Sigmund Freud, that mighty spirit in whose honour we are gathered together, founder of psychoanalysis as a general method of research and as a therapeutic technique, trod the steep path alone and independently, as physician and natural scientist, without knowing that reinforcement and encouragement lay to his hand in literature. He did not know Nietzsche, scattered throughout whose pages one finds premonitory flashes of truly Freudian insight; he did not know Novalis, whose romantic-biologic fantasies so often approach astonishingly close to analytic conceptions; he did not know Kierkegaard, whom he must have found profoundly sympathetic and encouraging for the Christian zeal which urged him on to psychological extremes; and, finally, he did not know Schopenhauer, the melancholy symphonist of a philosophy of the instinct, groping for change and redemption. Probably it must be so. By his unaided effort, without knowledge of

any previous intuitive achievement, he had methodically to follow
out the line of his own researches; the driving force of his activity was
probably increased by this very freedom from special advantage. And
we think of him as solitary – the attitude is inseparable from our earliest
picture of the man. Solitary in the sense of the word used by Nietzsche
in that ravishing essay 'What is the Meaning of Ascetic Ideals?' when
he characterises Schopenhauer as 'a genuine philosopher, a self-poised
mind, a man and gallant knight, stern-eyed, with the courage of his
own strength, who knows how to stand alone and not wait on the
beck and nod of superior officers'. In this guise of man and gallant
knight, a knight between Death and the Devil, I have been used to
picture to myself our psychologist of the unconscious, ever since his
figure first swam into my mental ken.

That happened late – much later than one might have expected,
considering the connection between this science and the poetic and
creative impulse in general and mine in particular. The connection,
the bond between them, is twofold: it consists first in a love of truth,
in a sense of truth, a sensitiveness and receptivity for truth's sweet and
bitter, which largely expresses itself in a psychological excitation, a
clarity of vision, to such an extent that the conception of truth actually
almost coincides with that of psychological perception and recognition.
And secondly it consists in an understanding of disease, a certain
affinity with it, outweighed by fundamental health, and an understanding of its productive significance.

As for the love of truth: the suffering, morally conditioned love of
truth *as psychology* – that has its origin in Nietzsche's lofty school,
where in fact the coincidence of 'truth' and 'psychological truth', of
the knower with the psychologist, is striking indeed. His proud truth-
fulness, his very conception of intellectual honesty, his conscious and
melancholy fearlessness in its service, his self-knowledge, self-cruci-
fixion – all this has psychological intention and bearing. Never shall I
forget the deepening, strengthening, formative effect upon my own
powers produced by my acquaintance with Nietzsche's psychological
agony. In *Tonio Kröger* the artist speaks of being 'sick of knowledge'.
That is true Nietzsche language; and the youth's melancholy has
reference to the Hamlet-like in Nietzsche's nature, in which his own
mirrored itself: a nature called to knowledge without being genuinely
born to it. These are the pangs and anguishes of youth, destined to be

lightened and tranquillised as years flowed by and brought ripeness
with them. But there has remained with me the desire for a psychological interpretation of knowledge and truth; I still equate them with
psychology and feel the psychological will to truth as a desire for
truth in general; still interpret psychology as truth in the most actual
and courageous sense of the word. One would call the tendency a
naturalistic one, I suppose, and ascribe it to a training in literary naturalism; it forms a precondition of receptivity for the natural science of the
psyche – in other words, for what is known as psychoanalysis.

I spoke of a second bond between that science and the creative
impulse: the understanding of disease, or, more precisely, of disease
as an instrument of knowledge. That, too, one may derive from
Nietzsche. He well knew what he owed to his morbid state, and on
every page he seems to instruct us that there is no deeper knowledge
without experience of disease, and that all heightened healthiness must
be achieved by the route of illness. This attitude too may be referred
to his experience; but it is bound up with the nature of the intellectual
man in general, of the creative artist in particular, yes, with the nature
of humanity and the human being, of which last of course the creative
artist is an extreme expression. '*L'humanité*,' says Victor Hugo, '*s'affirme
par l'infirmité.*' A saying which frankly and proudly admits the delicate
constitution of all higher humanity and culture and their connois-
seurship in the realm of disease. Man has been called '*das kranke Tier*'
because of the burden of strain and explicit difficulties laid upon him
by his position between nature and spirit, between angel and brute.
What wonder, then, that by the approach through abnormality we
have succeeded in penetrating most deeply into the darkness of human
nature; that the study of disease – that is to say, neurosis – has revealed
itself as a first-class technique of anthropological research?

The literary artist should be the last person to be surprised at the
fact. Sooner might he be surprised that he, considering his strong
general and individual tendency, should have so late become aware
of the close sympathetic relations which connected his own existence
with psychoanalytic research and the life-work of Sigmund Freud.
I realised this connection only at a time when his achievement was no
longer thought of as merely a therapeutic method, whether recognised
or disputed; when it had long since outgrown his purely medical
implications and become a world movement which penetrated into

every field of science and every domain of the intellect: literature, the history of art, religion and prehistory; mythology, folklore, pedagogy, and what not – thanks to the practical and constructive zeal of experts who erected a structure of more general investigation round the psychiatric and medical core. Indeed, it would be too much to say that I came to psychoanalysis. It came to me. Through the friendly interest that some younger workers in the field had shown in my work, from *Little Herr Freidemann* to *Death in Venice*, *The Magic Mountain*, and the *Joseph* novels, it gave me to understand that in my way I 'belonged'; it made me aware, as probably behoved it, of my own latent, preconscious sympathies; and when I began to occupy myself with the literature of psychoanalysis I recognised, arrayed in the ideas and the language of scientific exactitude, much that had long been familiar to me through my youthful mental experiences.

Perhaps you will kindly permit me to continue for a while in this autobiographical strain, and not take it amiss if instead of speaking of Freud I speak of myself. And indeed I scarcely trust myself to speak *about* him. What new thing could I hope to say? But I shall also, quite explicitly, be speaking in his honour in speaking of myself, in telling you how profoundly and peculiarly certain experiences decisive for my development prepared me for the Freudian experience. More than once, and in many places, I have confessed to the profound, even shattering impression made upon me as a young man by contact with the philosophy of Arthur Schopenhauer, to which then a monument was erected in the pages of *Buddenbrooks*. Here first, in the pessimism of a metaphysics already very strongly equipped on the natural-science side, I encountered the dauntless zeal for truth that stands for the moral aspect of the psychology of the unconscious. This metaphysics, in obscure revolt against centuries-old beliefs, preached the primacy of the instinct over mind and reason; it recognised the will as the core and the essential foundation of the world, in man as in all other created beings; and the intellect as secondary and accidental, servant of the will and its pale illuminant. This it preached not in malice, not in the anti-human spirit of the mind-hostile doctrines of today, but in the stern love of truth characteristic of the century which combated idealism out of love for the ideal. It was so sincere, that nineteenth century, that – through the mouth of Ibsen – it pronounced the lie, the lies of life, to be indispensable. Clearly there is a vast difference whether one

assents to a lie out of sheer hatred of truth and the spirit or for the sake
of the spirit, in bitter irony and anguished pessimism! Yet the distinction is not clear to everybody today.

Now, Freud, the psychologist of the unconscious, is a true son of the
century of Schopenhauer and Ibsen – he was born in the middle of it.
How closely related is his revolution to Schopenhauer's, not only in
its content, but also in its moral attitude! His discovery of the great
role played by the unconscious, the id, in the soul-life of man challenged
and challenges classical psychology, to which the consciousness and
the psyche are one and the same, as offensively as once Schopenhauer's
doctrine of the will challenged philosophical belief in reason and the
intellect. Certainly the early devotee of *The World as Will and Idea* is at
home in the admirable essay that is included in Freud's *New Introductory Essays in Psychoanalysis* under the title 'The Anatomy of the Mental
Personality'. It describes the soul-world of the unconscious, the id, in
language as strong, and at the same time in as cooly intellectual,
objective, and professional a tone, as Schopenhauer might have used
to describe his sinister kingdom of the will. 'The domain of the id,'
he says, 'is the dark, inaccessible part of our personality; the little that
we know of it we have learned through the study of dreams and of the
formation of neurotic symptoms.' He depicts it as a chaos, a melting-
pot of seething excitations. The id, he thinks, is, so to speak, open towards the somatic, and receives thence into itself compulsions which
there find psychic expression – in what substratum is unknown. From
these impulses it receives its energy; but it is not organised, produces
no collective will, merely the striving to achieve satisfaction for the
impulsive needs operating under the pleasure principle. In it no laws
of thought are valid, and certainly not the law of opposites. 'Contra-
dictory stimuli exist alongside each other without cancelling each other
out or even detracting from each other; at most they unite in compromise forms under the compulsion of the controlling economy for the
release of energy.' You perceive that this is a situation which, in the
historical experience of our own day, can take the upper hand with the
ego, with a whole mass-ego, thanks to a moral devastation which is
produced by worship of the unconscious, the glorification of its
dynamic as the only life-promoting force, the systematic glorification
of the primitive and irrational. For the unconscious, the id, is primitive
and irrational, is pure dynamic. It knows no values, no good or evil,

no morality. It even knows no time, no temporal flow, nor any effect of time upon its psychic process. 'Wish stimuli,' says Freud,

> which have never overpassed the id, and impressions which have been repressed into its depths, are virtually indestructible, they survive decade after decade as though they had just happened. They can only be recognised as belonging to the past, devalued and robbed of their charge of energy, by becoming conscious through the analytic procedure.

And he adds that therein lies pre-eminently the healing effect of analytic treatment. We perceive accordingly how antipathetic deep analysis must be to an ego that is intoxicated by a worship of the unconscious to the point of being in a condition of subterranean dynamic. It is only too clear and understandable that such an ego is deaf to analysis and that the name of Freud must not be mentioned in its hearing.

As for the ego itself, its situation is pathetic, well-nigh alarming. It is an alert, prominent, and enlightened little part of the id – much as Europe is a small and lively province of the greater Asia. The ego is that part of the id which became modified by contact with the outer world; equipped for the reception and preservation of stimuli; comparable to the integument with which any piece of living matter surrounds itself. A very perspicuous biological picture. Freud writes indeed a very perspicuous prose, he is an artist of thought, like Schopenhauer, and like him a writer of European rank. The relation with the outer world is, he says, decisive for the ego, it is the ego's task to represent the world to the id – for its good! For without regard for the superior power of the outer world the id, in its blind striving towards the satisfaction of its instincts, would not escape destruction. The ego takes cognisance of the outer world, it is mindful, it honourably tries to distinguish the objectively real from whatever is an accretion from its inward sources of stimulation. It is entrusted by the id with the lever of action; but between the impulse and the action it has interposed the delay of the thought-process, during which it summons experience to its aid and thus possesses a certain regulative superiority over the pleasure principle which rules supreme in the unconscious, correcting it by means of the principle of reality. But even so, how feeble it is! Hemmed in between the unconscious, the outer world, and what Freud calls the super-ego, it leads a pretty nervous and

anguished existence. Its own dynamic is rather weak. It derives its
energy from the id and in general has to carry out the latter's behests.
It is fain to regard itself as the rider and the unconscious as the horse.
But many a time it is ridden by the unconscious; and I take leave to
add what Freud's rational morality prevents him from saying, that
under some circumstances it makes more progress by this illegitimate
means.

But Freud's description of the id and the ego – is it not to a hair
Schopenhauer's description of the Will and the Intellect, a translation
of the latter's metaphysics into psychology? So he who had been ini-
tiated into the metaphysics of Schopenhauer and in Nietzsche tasted
the painful pleasure of psychology – he must needs have been filled
with a sense of recognition and familiarity when first, encouraged
thereto by its denizens, he entered the realms of psychoanalysis and
looked about him.

He found too that his new knowledge had a strange and strong
retroactive effect upon the old. After a sojourn in the world of Freud,
how differently, in the light of one's new knowledge, does one reread
the reflections of Schopenhauer, for instance his great essay 'Transcen-
dent Speculations on Apparent Design in the Fate of the Individual'!
And here I am about to touch upon the most profound and mysterious
point of contact between Freud's natural-scientific world and Schopenhauer's philosophic one. For the essay I have named, a marvel of
profundity and penetration, constitutes this point of contact. The
pregnant and mysterious idea there developed by Schopenhauer is
briefly this: that precisely as in a dream it is our own will that unconsciously appears as inexorable objective destiny, everything in it
proceeding out of ourselves and each of us being the secret theatre-
manager of our own dreams, so also in reality the great dream that a
single essence, the will itself, dreams with us all, our fate, may be the
product of our inmost selves, of our wills, and we are actually ourselves
bringing about what seems to be happening to us. I have only briefly
indicated here the content of the essay, for these representations are
winged with the strongest and most sweeping powers of suggestion.
But not only does the dream psychology which Schopenhauer calls
to his aid bear an explicitly psychoanalytic character, even to the presence of the sexual argument and paradigm; but the whole complexus
of thought is a philosophical anticipation of analytical conceptions,

to a quite astonishing extent. For, to repeat what I said in the beginning,
I see in the mystery of the unity of the ego and the world, of being
and happening, in the perception of the apparently objective and accidental as a matter of the soul's own contriving, the innermost core of
psychoanalytic theory.

And here there occurs to me a phrase from the pen of C. G. Jung, an
able but somewhat ungrateful scion of the Freudian school in his
significant introduction to the Tibetan *Book of the Dead*. It is so much
more direct, striking, impressive, and thus convincing,' he says, 'to
see how it happens to me than to see how I do it.' A bold, even an
extravagant statement, plainly betraying the calmness with which in a
certain school of psychology certain things are regarded which even
Schopenhauer considered prodigiously daring speculation. Would this
unmasking of the 'happening' as in reality 'doing' be conceivable without Freud? Never! It owes him everything. It is weighted down with
assumptions, it could not be understood, it could never have been
written, without all that analysis has brought to light about slips of
tongue and pen, the whole field of human error, the retreat into illness,
the psychology of accidents, the self-punishment compulsion – in
short, all the wizardry of the unconscious. Just as little, moreover,
would that close-packed sentence of Jung's, including its psychological premises, have been possible without Schopenhauer's adven-
turous pioneering speculation. Perhaps this is the moment, my friends,
to indulge on this festive occasion in a little polemic against Freud
himself. He does not esteem philosophy very highly. His scientific
exactitude does not permit him to regard it as a science. He reproaches
it with imagning that it can present a continuous and consistent picture of the world; with overestimating the objective value of logical
operations; with believing in intuitions as a source of knowledge and
with indulging in positively animistic tendencies, in that it believes in
the magic of words and the influence of thought upon reality. But
would philosophy really be thinking too highly of itself on these
assumptions? Has the world ever been changed by anything save by
thought and its magic vehicle the World? I believe that in actual fact
philosophy ranks before and above the natural sciences and that all
method and exactness serve its intuitions and its intellectual and historical will. In the last analysis it is always a matter of the *quod erat demon-
strandum*. Scientific freedom from assumptions is or should be a moral

fact. But intellectually it is, as Freud points out, probably an illusion. One might strain the point and say that science has never made a discovery without being authorised and encouraged thereto by philosophy.

All this by the way. But it is in line with my general intention to pause a little longer at the sentence that I quoted from Jung. In this essay and also as a general method which he uses by preference, Jung applies analytical evidence to form a bridge between Occidental thought and Oriental esoteric. Nobody has focused so sharply as he the Schopenhauer-Freud perception that 'the giver of all given conditions resides in ourselves – a truth which despite all evidence in the greatest as well as in the smallest things *never* becomes conscious, though it is only too often necessary, even indispensable, that it should be.' A great and costly change, he thinks, is needed before we understand how the world is 'given' by the nature of the soul; for man's animal nature strives against seeing himself as the maker of his own conditions. It is true that the East has always shown itself stronger than the West in the conquest of our animal nature, and we need not be surprised to hear that in its wisdom it conceives even the gods among the 'given conditions' originating from the soul and one with her, light and reflection of the human soul. This knowledge, which, according to the *Book of the Dead*, one gives to the deceased to accompany him on his way, is a paradox to the Occidental mind, conflicting with its sense of logic, which distinguishes between subject and object and refuses to have them coincide or make one proceed from the other. True, European mysticism has been aware of such attitudes, and Angelus Silesius said:

> I know that without me God cannot live a moment;
> If I am destroyed He must give up the ghost.

But on the whole a psychological conception of God, an idea of the godhead which is not pure condition, absolute reality, but one with the soul and bound up with it, must be intolerable to Occidental religious sense – it would be equivalent to abandoning the idea of God.

Yet religion – perhaps even etymologically – essentially implies a bond. In Genesis we have talk of the bond (covenant) between God and man, the psychological basis of which I have attempted to give in the mythological novel *Joseph and His Brothers*. Perhaps my hearers will be indulgent if I speak a little about my own work; there may be

some justification for introducing it here in this hour of formal en-
counter between creative literature and the psychoanalytic. It is strange
– and perhaps strange not only to me – that in this work there obtains
precisely that psychological theology which the scholar ascribes to
Oriental esoteric. This Abram is in a sense the father of God. He perceived and brought Him forth; His mighty qualities, ascribed to Him
by Abram, were probably His original possession, Abram was not
their inventor, yet in a sense he was, by virtue of his recognising them
and therewith, by taking thought, making them real. God's mighty
qualities – and thus God Himself – are indeed something objective
exterior to Abram; but at the same time they are in him and of him
as well; the power of his own soul is at moments scarcely to be distinguished from them, it consciously interpenetrates and fuses with
them – and such is the origin of the bond which then the Lord strikes
with Abram, as the explicit confirmation of an inward fact. The bond,
it is stated, is made in the interest of both, to the end of their common
sanctification. Need human and need divine here entwine until it is
hard to say whether it was the human or the divine that took the
initiative. In any case the arrangement shows that the holiness of man
and the holiness of God constituted a twofold process, one part being
most intimately bound up with the other. Wherefore else, one asks,
should there be a bond at all?

The soul as 'giver of the given' – yes, my friends I am well aware
that in the novel this conception reaches an ironic pitch which is not
authorised either in Oriental wisdom or in psychological perception.
But there is something thrilling about the unconscious and only
later discovered harmony. Shall I call it the power of suggestion?
But sympathy would be a better word: a kind of intellectual affinity
of which naturally psychoanalysis was earlier aware than was I and
which proceeded out of those literary appreciations which I owed to it
at an earlier stage. The latest of these was an offprint of an article
that appeared in *Imago* written by a Viennese scholar of the Freudian
school under the title 'On the Psychology of the Older School of
Biography'. The rather dry title gives no indication of the remarkable
contents. The writer shows how the older and simpler type of biography and in particular the written lives of artists nourished and
conditioned by popular legend and tradition assimilate as it were,
the life of the subject to the conventionalised stock-in-trade of bio-

graphy in general thus imparting a sort of sanction to their own performance and establishing its genuineness; making it authentic in the
sense of 'as it always was' and 'as it has been written'. For man sets
store by recognition he likes to find the old in the new, the typical
in the individual. From that recognition he draws a sense of the familiar
in life, whereas if it painted itself as entirely new, singular in time and
space, without any possibility of resting upon the known, it could only
bewilder and alarm. The question, then, which is raised by the essay,
is this: can any line be sharply and unequivocally drawn between
the formal stock-in-trade of legendary biography and the characteristics of the single personality – in other words, between the typical
and the individual? A question negatived by its very statement. For
the truth is that life is a mingling of the individual elements and the
formal stock-in-trade; a mingling in which the individual, as it were,
only lifts his head above the formal and impersonal elements. Much
that is extra-personal, much unconscious identification, much that is
conventional and schematic, is none the less decisive for the experience
not only of the artist but of the human being in general. 'Many of us,'
says the writer of the article, 'live today a biographical type, the destiny
of a class or rank or calling. The freedom in the shaping of the human
being's life is obviously connected with that bond which we term
lived *vita*.' And then, to my delight, but scarcely to my surprise,
he begins to cite from *Joseph*, the fundamental motif of which he says
is precisely this idea of the 'lived life', life as succession, as a moving
in others' steps, as identification – such as Joseph's teacher, Eliezer,
practises with droll solemnity. For in him time is cancelled and all the
Eliezers of the past gather to shape the Eliezer of the present, so that
he speaks in the first person of that Eliezer who was Abram's servant,
though he was far from being the same man.

I must admit that I find the train of thought extraordinarily convincing. The essay indicates the precise point at which the psychological interest passes over into the mythical. It makes it clear that the
typical is actually the mythical, and that one may as well say 'lived
myth' as 'lived life'. But the mythus as lived is the epic idea embodied
in my novel; and it is plain to me that when as a novelist I took the
step in my subject-matter from the bourgeois and individual to the
mythical and typical my personal connection with the analytic field
passed into its acute stage. The mythical interest is as native to psycho-

analysis as the psychological interest is to all creative writing. Its penetration into the childhood of the individual soul is at the same time a penetration into the childhood of mankind, into the primitive and mythical. Freud has told us that for him all natural science, medicine, and psychotherapy were a lifelong journey round and back to the early passion of his youth for the history of mankind, for the origins of religion and morality – an interest which at the height of his career broke out to such magnificent effect in *Totem and Taboo*. The word *Tiefenpsychologie* ('deep' psychology) has a temporal significance; the primitive foundations of the human soul are likewise primitive time, they are those profound time-sources where the myth has its home and shapes the primeval norms and forms of life. For the myth is the foundation of life; it is the timeless schema, the pious formula into which life flows when it reproduces its traits out of the unconscious. Certainly when a writer has acquired the habit of regarding life as mythical and typical there comes a curious heightening of his artist temper, a new refreshment to his perceiving and shaping powers, which otherwise occurs much later in life; for while in the life of the human race the mythical is an early and primitive stage, in the life of the individual it is a late and mature one. What is gained is an insight into the higher truth depicted in the actual; a smiling knowledge of the eternal, the ever-being and authentic; a knowledge of the schema in which and according to which the supposed individual lives, unaware, in his naive belief in himself as unique in space and time, of the extent to which his life is but formula and repetition and his path marked out for him by those who trod it before him. His character is a mythical role which the actor just emerged from the depths to the light plays in the illusion that it is his own and unique, that he, as it were, has invented it all himself, with a dignity and security of which his supposed unique individuality in time and space is not the source, but rather which he creates out of his deeper consciousness in order that something which was once founded and legitimised shall again be represented and once more for good or ill, whether nobly or basely, in any case after its own kind conduct itself according to pattern. Actually, if his existence consisted merely in the unique and the present, he would not know how to conduct himself at all; he would be confused, helpless, unstable in his own self-regard, would not know which foot to put foremost or what sort of face to put on. His dignity and security lie all unconsciously in the fact that with him something timeless has once more emerged into the light and become present; it is a mythical value added to the otherwise poor and valueless single character; it is native worth, because its origin lies in the unconscious.

Such is the gaze which the mythically oriented artist bends upon the phenomena about him – an ironic and superior gaze, as you can see, for the mythical knowledge resides in the gazer and not in that at which he gazes. But let us suppose that the mythical point of view could become subjective; that it could pass over into the active ego and become conscious there, proudly and darkly yet joyously, of its recurrence and its typicality, could celebrate its role and realise its own value exclusively in the knowledge that it was a fresh incarnation of the traditional upon earth. One might say that such a phenomenon alone could be the 'lived myth'; nor should we think that it is anything novel or unknown. The life in the myth, life as a sacred repetition, is a historical form of life, for the man of ancient times lived thus. An instance is the figure of the Egyptian Cleopatra, which is Ishtar, Astarte, Aphrodite in person. Bachofen, in his description of the cult of Bacchus, the Dionysiac religion, regards the Egyptian queen as the consummate picture of a Dionysiac *stimula;* and according to Plutarch it was far more her erotic intellectual culture than her physical charms that entitled her to represent the female as developed into the earthly embodiment of Aphrodite. But her Aphrodite nature, her role of Hathor-Isis, is not only objective, not only a treatment of her by Plutarch or Bachofen; it was the content of her subjective existence as well, she lived the part. This we can see by the manner of her death: she is supposed to have killed herself by laying an asp upon her bosom. But the snake was the familiar of Ishtar, the Egyptian Isis, who is represented clad in a garment of scales; also there exists a statuette of Ishtar holding a snake to her bosom. So that if Cleopatra's death was as the legend represents, the manner of it was a manifestation of her mythical ego. Moreover, did she not adopt the falcon hood of the goddess Isis and adorn herself with the insignia of Hathor, the cow's horns with the cresent moon between? And name her two children by Mark Antony Helios and Selene? No doubt she was a very significant figure indeed – significant in the antique sense, that she was well aware who she was and in whose footsteps she trod!

The ego of antiquity and its consciousness of itself were different from our own, less exclusive, less sharply defined, It was, as it were, open behind; it received much from the past and by repeating it gave it presentness again. The Spanish scholar Ortega y Gasset puts it that the man of antiquity, before he did anything, took a step backwards, like the bull-fighter who leaps back to deliver the mortal thrust. He searched the past for a pattern into which he might slip as into a diving-bell, and being thus at once disgusied and protected might rush upon his present problem. Thus his life was in a sense a reanimation, an archaising attitude. But it is just this life as reanimation that is the life as myth. Alexander walked in the footsteps of Miltiades; the ancient biographers of Caesar were convinced, rightly or wrongly, that he took Alexander as his prototype. But such 'imitation' meant far more than we mean by the word today. It was a mythical identification, peculiarly familiar to antiquity; but it is operative far into modern times, and at all times is psychically possible. How often have we not been told that the figure of Napoleon was cast in the antique mould! He regretted that the mentality of the time forbade him to give himself out for the son of Jupiter Ammon, in imitation of Alexander. But we need not doubt that – at least at the period of his Eastern exploits – he mythically confounded himself with Alexander; while after he turned his face westwards he is said to have declared: 'I am Charlemagne.' Note that: not 'I am like Charlemagne' or 'My situation is like Charlemagne's', but quite simply: 'I am he'. That is the formulation of the myth. Life, then – at any rate, significant life – was in ancient times the reconstitution of the myth in flesh and blood; it referred to and appealed to the myth; only through it, through reference to the past, could it approve itself as genuine and significant. The myth is the legitimisation of life; only through and in it does life finds self-awareness, sanction, consecration. Cleopatra fulfilled her Aphrodite character even unto death – and can one live and die more significantly or worthily than in the celebration of the myth? We have only to think of Jesus and His life, which was lived in order that that which was written might be fulfilled. It is not easy to distinguish between His own consciousness and the conventionalisations of the Evangelists. But His word on the Cross, about the ninth hour, that '*Eli, Eli, lama sabachthani*' was evidently not in the least an outburst of despair and disillusionment; but on the contrary a lofty messianic sense of self. For the phrase is not original, not a spontaneous outcry. It stands at the beginning of the

Twenty-second Psalm, which from one end to the other is an announce-
ment of the Messiah. Jesus was quoting, and the quotation meant: 'Yes,
it is I!' Precisely thus did Cleopatra quote when she took the asp to
her breast to die; and again the quotation meant: 'Yes, it is I!'

Let us consider for a moment the word 'celebration' which I used
in this connection. It is a pardonable, even a proper usage. For life
in the myth, life, so to speak, in quotation, is a kind of celebration,
in that it is a making present of the past, it becomes a religious act, the
performance by a celebrant of a prescribed procedure; it becomes a
feast. For a feast is an anniversary, a renewal of the past in the present.
Every Christmas the world-saving Babe is born again on earth, to
suffer, to die, and to arise. The feast is the abrogation of time, an event,
a solemn narrative being played out conformably to an immemorial
pattern; the events in it take place not for the first time, but ceremonially
according to the prototype. It achieves presentness as feasts do, recur-
ring in time with their phases and hours following on each other in
time as they did in the original occurrence. In antiquity each feast
was essentially a dramatic performance, a mask; it was the scenic
reproduction, with priests as actors, of stories about the gods – as for
instance the life and sufferings of Osiris. The Christian Middle Ages
had their mystery play, with heaven, earth, and the torments of hell –
just as we have it later in Goethe's *Faust*; they had their carnival
farce, their folk-mime. The artist eye has a mythical slant upon life,
which makes it look like a farce, like a theatrical performance of a
prescribed feast, like a Punch and Judy epic, wherein mythical character puppets reel off a plot abiding from past time and now again
present in a jest. It only lacks that this mythical slant pass over and
become subjective in the performers themselves, become a festival
and mythical consciousness of part and play, for an epic to be produced
such as that in the first volume of the *Joseph and His Brothers* series,
particularly in the chapter 'The Great Hoaxing'. There a mythical
recurrent farce is tragicomically played by personages all of whom
well know in whose steps they tread: Isaac, Esau, and Jacob; and who
act out the cruel and grotesque tale of how Esau the Red is led by the
nose and cheated of his birthright to the huge delight of all the by-
standers. Joseph too is another such celebrant of life; with charming
mythological hocus-pocus he enacts in his own person the Tammuz–
Osiris myth, 'bringing to pass' anew the story of the mangled, buried,

and arisen god, playing his festival game with that which mysteriously and secretly shapes life out of its own depths – the unconscious. The mystery of the metaphysician and psychologist, that the soul is the giver of all given conditions, becomes in Joseph easy, playful, blithe – like a consummately artistic performance by a fencer or juggler. It reveals his *infantile* nature – and the word I have used betrays how closely though seeming to wander so far afield, we have kept to the subject of our evening's homage.

Infantilism – in other words, regression to childhood – what a role this genuinely psychoanalytic element plays in all our lives! What a large share it has in shaping the life of a human being; operating, indeed, in just the way I have described: as mythical identification, as survival, as a treading in footprints already made! The bond with the father, the imitation of the father, the game of being the father, and the transference to father-substitute pictures of a higher and more developed type – how these infantile traits work upon the life of the individual to mark and shape it! I use the word 'shape', for to me in all seriousness the happiest, most pleasurable element of what we call education (*Bildung*), the shaping of the human being, is just this power-ful influence of admiration and love, this childish identification with a father-image elected out of profound affinity. The artist in particular, a passionately childlike and play-possessed being, can tell us of the mysterious yet after all obvious effect of such infantile imitation upon his own life, his productive conduct of a career which after all is often nothing but a reanimation of the hero under very different temporal and personal conditions and with very different, shall we say childish means. The *imitatio* Goethe, with its Werther and Wilhelm Meister stages, its old-age period of *Faust* and *Diwan*, can still shape and mythi-cally mould the life of an artist – rising out of his unconscious, yet playing over – as is the artist way – into a smiling, childlike, and pro-found awareness.

The Joseph of the novel is an artist, playing with his *imitatio dei* upon the unconscious string; and I know not how to express the feelings which possess me – something like a joyful sense of divination of the future – when I indulge in this encouragement of the unconscious to play, to make itself fruitful in a serious product, in a narrational meet-ing of psychology and myth, which is at the same time a celebration of the meeting between poetry and analysis.

And now this word 'future': I have used it in the title of my address, because it is this idea, the idea of the future, that I involuntarily like best to connect with the name of Freud. But even as I have been speaking I have been asking myself whether I have not been guilty of a cause of confusion; whether – from what I have said up to now – a better title might not have been something like 'Freud and the Myth'. And yet I rather cling to the combination of name and word and I should like to justify and make clear its relation to what I have so far said. I make bold to believe that in that novel so kin to the Freudian world, making as it does the light of psychology play upon the myth, there lie hidden seeds and elements of a new and coming sense of our humanity. And no less firmly do I hold that we shall one day recognise in Freud's life-work the cornerstone for the building of a new anthropology and therewith of a new structure, to which many stones are being brought up today, which shall be the future dwelling of a wiser and freer humanity. This physicianly psychologist will, I make no doubt at all, be honoured as the path-finder towards a humanism of the future, which we dimly divine and which will have experienced much that the earlier humanism knew not of. It will be a humanism standing in a different relation to the powers of the lower world, the unconscious, the id: a relation bolder, freer, blither, productive of a riper art than any possible in our neurotic, fear-ridden, hate-ridden world. Freud is of the opinion that the significance of psychoanalysis as a science of the unconscious will in the future far outrank its value as a therapeutic method. But even as a science of the unconscious it is a therapeutic method, in the grand style, a method overarching the individual case. Call this, if you choose, a poet's utopia: but the thought is after all not unthinkable that the resolution of our great fear and our great hate, their conversion into a different relation to the unconscious which shall be more the artist's, more ironic and yet not necessarily irreverent, may one day be due to the healing effect of this very science.

The analytic revelation is a revolutionary force. With it a blithe scepticism has come into the world, a mistrust that unmasks all the schemes and subterfuges of our own souls. Once roused and on the alert, it cannot be put to sleep again. It infiltrates life, undermines its raw naïveté, takes from it the strain of its own ignorance, de-emotionalises it, as it were, inculcates the taste for understatement, as the English call it – for the deflated rather than for the inflated word, for the cult which exerts its influence by moderation, by modesty. Modesty – what a beautiful word! In the German (*Bescheidenheit*) it originally had to do with knowing and only later got its present meaning; while the Latin word from which the English comes means a way of doing – in short, both together give us almost the sense of the French *savoir faire* – to know how to do. May we hope that this may be the fundamental temper of that more blithely objective and peaceful world which the science of the unconscious may be called to usher in?

Its mingling of the pioneer with the physicianly spirit justifies such a hope. Freud once called his theory of dreams 'a bit of scientific new-found land won from superstition and mysticism'. The word 'won' expresses the colonising spirit and significance of his work. 'Where id was, shall be ego,' he epigrammatically says. And he calls analysis a cultural labour comparable to the draining of the Zuider Zee. Almost in the end the traits of the venerable man merge into the lineaments of the grey-haired Faust, whose spirit urges him

> to shut the imperious sea from the shore away,
> Set narrower bounds to the broad water's waste.
>
> Then open I to many millions space
> Where they may live, not safe-secure, but free
> And active. And such a busy swarming I would see
> Standing amid free folk on a free soil.

The free folk are the people of a future freed from fear and hate, and ripe for peace.

SOURCE: Thomas Mann, *Essays of Three Decades* (1965).

LUDWIG WITTGENSTEIN

Conversations on Freud (1943-6)

IN these discussions Wittgenstein was critical of Freud. But he was also bringing out how much there is in what Freud says about the notion of 'dream symbolism', for instance, or the suggestion that in dreaming I am – in some sense – 'saying something'. He was trying to separate what is valuable in Freud from that 'way of thinking' which he wanted to combat.

He told me that when he was in Cambridge before 1914 he had thought psychology a waste of time. (Although he had not ignored it. I heard him explain the Weber-Fechner law to a student in a way that cannot have come simply from reading Meinong's article or from discussions with Russell.) 'Then some years later I happened to read something by Freud, and I sat up in surprise. Here was someone who had something to say.' I think this was soon after 1919. And for the rest of his life Freud was one of the few authors he thought worth reading. He would speak of himself – at the period of these discussions – as 'a disciple of Freud' and 'a follower of Freud'.

He admired Freud for the observations and suggestions in his writings; for 'having something to say' even where, in Wittgenstein's view, he was wrong. On the other hand, he thought the enormous influence of psychoanalysis in Europe and America was harmful – 'although it will take a long time before we lose our subservience to it'. To learn from Freud you have to be critical; and psychoanalysis generally prevents this.

I spoke of the harm it does to writing when an author tries to bring psychoanalysis into the story. 'Of course,' he said, 'There's nothing worse.' He was ready to illustrate what Freud meant by referring to a story; but then the story had been written independently. Once when Wittgenstein was recounting something Freud had said and the advice he had given someone, one of us said that this advice did not seem

very wise. 'Oh certainly not,' said Wittgenstein. 'But wisdom is
something I never would expect from Freud. Cleverness, certainly;
but not wisdom.' Wisdom was something he did admire in his favourite
story writers – in Gottfried Keller, for instance. The kind of criticism
which would help in studying Freud, would have to go deep; and it is
not common.

RUSH RHEES

WITTGENSTEIN (notes by R. R. after a conversation, Summer 1942).
 When we are studying psychology we may feel there is something
unsatisfactory, some difficulty about the whole subject or study –
because we are taking physics as our ideal science. We think of formulat-
ing laws as in physics. And then we find we cannot use the same sort
of 'metric', the same ideas of measurement as in physics. This is especially
clear when we try to describe appearances: the least noticeable differences of colours; the least noticeable differences of length, and so on.
Here it seems that we cannot say: 'If A = B, and B = C, then A = C,'
for instance. And this sort of trouble goes all through the subject.
 Or suppose you want to speak of causality in the operation of feelings. 'Determinism applies to the mind as truly as to physical things.'
This is obscure because when we think of causal laws in physical
things we think of *experiments*. We have nothing like this in connexion
with feelings and motivation. And yet psychologists want to say:
'There *must* be some law' – although no law has been found. (Freud:
'Do you want to say, gentlemen, that changes in mental phenomena
are guided by *chance*?') Whereas to me the fact that there *aren't* actually
any such laws seems important.
 Freud's theory of dreams. He wants to say that whatever happens in
a dream will be found to be connected with some wish which analysis
can bring to light. But this procedure of free association and so on is
queer, because Freud never shows how we know where to stop –
where is the right solution. Sometimes he says that the right solution,
or the right analysis, is the one which satisfies the patient. Sometimes
he says that the doctor knows what the right solution or analysis of the
dream is whereas the patient doesn't: the doctor can say that the patient
is wrong.
 The reason why he calls one sort of analysis the right one, does
not seem to be a matter of evidence. Neither is the proposition that

hallucinations, and so dreams, are wish fulfilments. Suppose a starving man has an hallucination of food. Freud wants to say the hallucination of anything requires tremendous energy: it is not something that could normally happen, but the energy is provided in the exceptional circumstances where a man's wish for food is overpowering. This is a *speculation*. It is the sort of explanation we are inclined to accept. It is not put forward as a result of detailed examination of varieties of hallucinations.

Freud in his analysis provides explanations which many people are inclined to accept. He emphasises that people are *dis*-inclined to accept them. But if the explanation is one which people are disinclined to accept, it is highly probable that it is also one which they are *inclined* to accept. And this is what Freud had actually brought out. Take Freud's view that anxiety is always a repetition in some way of the anxiety we felt at birth. He does not establish this by reference to evidence – for he could not do so. But it is an idea which has a marked attraction. It has the attraction which mythological explanations have, explanations which say that this is all a repetition of something that has happened before. And when people do accept or adopt this, then certain things seem much clearer and easier for them. So it is with the notion of the unconscious also. Freud does claim to find evidence in memories brought to light in analysis. But at a certain stage it is not clear how far such memories are due to the analyst. In any case, do they show that the anxiety was necessarily a repetition of the original anxiety?

Symbolising in dreams. The idea of a dream language. Think of recognising a painting as a dream. I (L. W.) was once looking at an exhibition of paintings by a young woman artist in Vienna. There was one painting of a bare room, like a cellar. Two men in top hats were sitting on chairs. Nothing else. And the title: 'Besuch' ('Visit'). When I saw this I said at once, 'This is a dream.' (My sister described the picture to Freud, and he said, 'Oh yes, that is quite a common dream' – connected with virginity.) Note that the title is what clinches it as a dream – by which I do not mean that anything like this was dreamt by the painter while asleep. You would not say of *every* painting, 'This is a dream'. And this does show that there is something like a dream language.

Freud mentions various symbols: top hats are regularly phallic symbols, wooden things like tables are women, etc. His historical explanation of these symbols is absurd. We might say it is not needed anyway: it is the most natural thing in the world that a table should be that sort of symbol.

But dreaming – using this sort of language – although it *may* be used to refer to a woman or to a phallus, may *also* be used not to refer to that at all. If some activity is shown to be carried out often for a certain purpose – striking someone to inflict pain – then a hundred to one it is also carried out under other circumstances *not* for that purpose. He may just want to strike him without thinking of inflicting pain at all. The fact that we are inclined to recognise the hat as a phallic symbol does not mean that the artist was necessarily referring to a phallus in any way when she painted it.

Consider the difficulty that if a symbol in a dream is not understood, it does not seem to be a symbol at all. So why call it one? But suppose I have a dream and accept a certain interpretation of it. *Then* – when I superimpose the interpretation on the dream – I can say, 'Oh yes, the table obviously corresponds to the woman, this to that, etc.'

I might be making scratches on the wall. It seems in a way like writing, but it is not a writing which either I or anyone else would recognise or understand. So we say I'm doodling. Then an analyst begins to ask me questions, trace associations and so on; and we come to an explanation of why I'm doing this. We may then correlate various scratches which I make with various elements in the interpretation. And we may then refer to the doodling as a kind of writing, as using a kind of language, although it was not understood by anyone.

Freud is constantly claiming to be scientific. But what he gives is *speculation* – something prior even to the formation of an hypothesis.

He speaks of overcoming resistance. One 'instance' is deluded by another 'instance'. (In the sense in which we speak of 'a court of higher instance' with authority to overrule the judgement of the lower court. R.R.) The analyst is supposed to be stronger, able to combat and overcome the delusion of the instance. But there is no way of showing that the whole result of analysis may not be 'delusion'. It is something which people are inclined to accept and which makes it easier for them to go certain ways: it makes certain ways of behaving and thinking natural for them. They have given up one way of thinking and adopted another.

Can we say we have laid bare the essential nature of mind? 'Concept formation'. Couldn't the whole thing have been differently treated?

WITTGENSTEIN (notes following conversations in 1943; Rush Rhees). DREAMS. The interpretation of dreams. Symbolism.

When Freud speaks of certain images – say the image of a hat – as symbols, or when he says the image 'means' so and so, he is speaking of interpretation; and of what the dreamer can be brought to accept as an interpretation.

It is characteristic of dreams that often they seem to the dreamer to call for an interpretation. One is hardly ever inclined to write down a day dream, or recount it to someone else, or to ask 'What does it mean?' But dreams do seem to have something puzzling and in a special way interesting about them – so that we want an interpretation of them. (They were often regarded as messages.)

There seems to be something in dream images that has a certain resemblance to the signs of a language. As a series of marks on paper or on sand might have. There might be no mark which we recognised as a conventional sign in any alphabet we knew, and yet we might have a strong feeling that they must be a language of some sort: that they mean something. There is a cathedral in Moscow with five spires. On each of these there is a different sort of curving configuration. One gets the strong impression that these different shapes and arrangements must mean something.

When a dream is interpreted we might say that it is fitted into a context in which it ceases to be puzzling. In a sense the dreamer re-dreams his dream in surroundings such that its aspect changes. It is as though we were presented with a bit of canvas on which were painted a hand and a part of a face and certain other shapes, arranged in a puzzling and incongruous manner. Suppose this bit is surrounded by considerable stretches of blank canvas, and that we now paint in forms – say an arm, a trunk, etc. – leading up to and fitting on to the shapes on the original bit; and that the result is that we say: 'Ah, now I see why it is like that, how it all comes to be arranged in that way, and what these various bits are . . .' and so on.

Mixed up with the shapes on the original bit of canvas there might be certain forms of which we should say that they do not join on to further figures in the wider canvas; they are not parts of bodies or trees, etc., but bits of writing. We might say this of a snake, perhaps, or a hat or some such. (These would be like the configurations of the Moscow cathedral.)

What is done in interpreting dreams is not all of one sort. There is a work of interpretation which, so to speak, still belongs to the dream itself. In considering what a dream is, it is important to consider what happens to it, the way its aspect changes when it is brought into relation with other things remembered, for instance. On first awaking a dream may impress one in various ways. One may be terrified and anxious; or when one has written the dream down one may have a certain sort of thrill, feel a very lively interest in it, feel intrigued by it. If one now remembers certain events in the previous day and connects what was dreamed with these, this already makes a difference, changes the aspect of the dream. If reflecting on the dream then leads one to remember certain things in early childhood, this will give it a different aspect still. And so on. (All this is connected with what was said about dreaming the dream over again. It still belongs to the dream, in a way.)

On the other hand, one might form an hypothesis. On reading the report of the dream, one might predict that the dreamer can be brought to recall such and such memories. And this hypothesis might or might not be verified. This might be called a scientific treatment of the dream.

Freier Einfall and wish fulfilments. There are various criteria for the right interpretation: e.g., (1) what the analyst says or predicts, on the basis of his previous experience; (2) what the dreamer is led to by *freier Einfall*. It would be interesting and important if these two generally coincided. But it would be queer to claim (as Freud seems to) that they *must always* coincide.

What goes on in *freier Einfall* is probably conditioned by a whole host of circumstances. There seems to be no reason for saying that it must be conditioned only by the sort of wish in which the analyst is interested and of which he has reason to say that it must have been playing a part. If you want to complete what seems to be a fragment of a picture, you might be advised to give up trying to think hard about what is the most likely way the picture went, and instead simply to stare at the picture and make whatever dash first comes into your mind, without thinking. This might in many cases be very fruitful advice to give. But it would be astonishing if it *always* produced the

best results. What dashes you make are likely to be conditioned by
everything that is going on about you and within you. And if I knew one
of the factors present, this could not tell me with certainty what dash
you were going to make.

To say that dreams are wish fulfilments is very important chiefly
because it points to the sort of interpretation that is wanted – the sort
of things that would be an interpretation of a dream. As contrasted
with an interpretation which said that dreams were simply memories
of what had happened, for instance. (We don't feel that memories
call for an interpretation in the same way as we feel this about dreams.)
And some dreams obviously are wish fulfilments; such as the sexual
dreams of adults, for instance. But it seems muddled to say that *all*
dreams are hallucinated wish fulfilments. (Freud very commonly gives
what we might call a sexual interpretation. But it is interesting that
among all the reports of dreams which he gives, there is not a single
example of a straightforward sexual dream. Yet these are common as
rain.) Partly because this doesn't seem to fit with dreams that spring
from fear rather than from longing. Partly because the majority of
dreams Freud considers have to be regarded as *camouflaged* wish fulfilments; and in this case they simply don't fulfil the wish. Ex hypo-
thesi the wish is not allowed to be fulfilled, and something else is
hallucinated instead. If the wish is cheated in this way, then the dream
can hardly be called a fulfilment of it. Also it becomes impossible to
say whether it is the wish or the censor that is cheated. Apparently
both are, and the result is that neither is satisfied. So that, the dream is
not an hallucinated satisfaction of anything.

It is probable that there are many different sorts of dreams, and that
there is no single line of explanation for all of them. Just as there are
many different sorts of jokes. Or just as there are many different sorts
of language.

Freud was influenced by the nineteenth century idea of dynamics –
an idea which has influenced the whole treatment of psychology.
He wanted to find some one explanation which would show what
dreaming is. He wanted to find the *essence* of dreaming. And he would
have rejected any suggestion that he might be partly right but not
altogether so. If he was partly wrong, that would have meant for him
that he was wrong altogether – that he had not really found the essence
of dreaming.

WITTGENSTEIN. (Notes following conversations, 1943. R.R.)

Whether a dream is a thought. Whether dreaming is thinking about something.

Suppose you look on a dream as a kind of language. A way of saying something, or a way of symbolising something. There might be a regular symbolism, not necessarily alphabetical – it might be like Chinese, say. We might then find a way of translating this symbolism into the language of ordinary speech, ordinary thoughts. But then the translation ought to be possible both ways. It ought to be possible by employing the same technique to translate ordinary thoughts into dream language. As Freud recognises, this never is done and cannot be done. So we might question whether dreaming is a way of thinking something, whether it is a language at all.

Obviously there are certain similarities with language.

Suppose there were a picture in a comic paper, dated shortly after the last war. It might contain one figure of which you would say it was obviously a caricature of Churchill, another figure marked somehow with a hammer and sickle so that you would say it was obviously supposed to be Russia. Suppose the title of the picture was lacking. Still you might be sure that, in view of two figures mentioned, the whole picture was obviously trying to make some point about the political situation at that time.

The question is whether you would always be justified in assuming that there is some one joke or some one point which is *the* point which the cartoon is making. Perhaps even the picture as a whole has no 'right interpretation' at all. You might say: 'There are indications – such as the two figures mentioned – which suggest that it has.' And I might answer that perhaps these indications are all that there is. Once you have got an interpretation of these two figures, there may be no ground for saying that there *must* be an interpretation of the whole thing or of every detail of it on similar lines.

The situation may be similar in dreams.

Freud would ask: 'What made you hallucinate that situation at all?' One might answer that there need not have been anything that *made* me hallucinate it.

Freud seems to have certain prejudices about when an interpretation could be regarded as complete – and so about when it still requires completion, when further interpretation is needed. Suppose someone were ignorant of the tradition among sculptors of making busts. If he then came upon the finished bust of some man, he might say that obviously this is a fragment and that there must have been other parts belonging to it, making it a whole body.

Suppose you recognised certain things in the dream which can be interpreted in the Freudian manner. Is there any ground at all for assuming that there must be an interpretation for everything else in the dream as well? that it makes any sense to ask what is the right interpretation of the other things there?

Freud asks, 'Are you asking me to believe that there is anything which happens without a cause?' But this means nothing. If under 'cause' you include things like physiological causes, then we know nothing about these, and in any case they are not relevant to the question of interpretation. Certainly you can't argue from Freud's question to the proposition that everything in the dream must have a cause in the sense of some past event with which it is connected by association in that way.

Suppose we were to regard a dream as a kind of game which the dreamer played. (And by the way, there is no one cause or one reason why children always play. This is where theories of play generally go wrong.) There might be a game in which paper figures were put together to form a story, or at any rate were somehow assembled. The materials might be collected and stored in a scrap-book, full of pictures and anecdotes. The child might then take various bits from the scrap-book to put into the construction; and he might take a considerable picture because it had something in it which he wanted and he might just include the rest because it was there.

Compare the question of why we dream and why we write stories. Not everything in the story is allegorical. What would be meant by trying to explain why he has written just that story in just that way?

There is no one reason why people talk. A small child babbles often just for the pleasure of making noises. This is also one reason why adults talk. And there are countless others.

Freud seems constantly to be influenced by the thought that an hallucination is something requiring a tremendous mental force – *seelische Kraft*. 'Ein Traum findet sich niemals mit Halbheiten ab.' And he thinks that the only force strong enough to produce the hallucinations of dreams is to be found in the deep wishes of early childhood. One might question this. Supposing it is true that hallucinations in waking state require an extraordinary mental force – why should not dream hallucinations be the perfectly normal thing in sleep, not requiring any extraordinary force at all?

(Compare the question: 'Why do we punish criminals? Is it from a desire for revenge? Is it in order to prevent a repetition of the crime?' And so on. The truth is that there is no one reason. There is the institution of punishing criminals. Different people support this for different reasons, and for different reasons in different cases and at different times. Some people support it out of a desire for revenge, some perhaps out of a desire for justice, some out of a wish to prevent a repetition of the crime, and so on. And so punishments are carried out.)

WITTGENSTEIN (notes following conversation, 1946 R.R.)

I have been going through Freud's 'Interpretation of Dreams' with H. And it has made me feel how much this whole way of thinking wants combating.

If I take any one of the dream reports (reports of his own dreams) which Freud gives, I can by the use of free association arrive at the same results as those he reaches in his analysis – although it was not my dream. And the association will proceed through my own experiences and so on.

The fact is that whenever you are preoccupied with something, with some trouble or with some problem which is a big thing in your life – as sex is, for instance – then no matter what you start from, the association will lead finally and inevitably back to that same theme. Freud remarks on how, after the analysis of it, the dream appears so very logical. And of course it does.

You could start with any of the objects on this table – which certainly are not put there through your dream activity – and you could find that they all could be connected in a pattern like that; and the pattern would be logical in the same way.

One may be able to discover certain things about oneself by this sort of free association, but it does not explain why the dream occurred.

Freud refers to various ancient myths in these connexions, and claims that his researches have now explained how it came about that anybody should think or propound a myth of that sort.

Whereas in fact Freud has done something different. He has not given a scientific explanation of the ancient myth. What he has done is to propound a new myth. The attractiveness of the suggestion, for instance, that all anxiety is a repetition of the anxiety of the birth trauma, is just the attractiveness of a mythology. 'It is all the outcome of something that happened long ago.' Almost like referring to a totem.

Much the same could be said of the notion of an 'Urszene'. This often has the attractiveness of giving a sort of tragic pattern to one's life. It is all the repetition of the same pattern which was settled long ago. Like a tragic figure carrying out the decrees under which the fates had placed him at birth. Many people have, at some period, serious trouble in their lives – so serious as to lead to thoughts of suicide. This is likely to appear to one as something nasty, as a situation which is too foul to be a subject of a tragedy. And it may then be an immense relief if it can be shown that one's life has the pattern rather of a tragedy – the tragic working out and repetition of a pattern which was determined by the primal scene.

There is of course the difficulty of determining what scene is the primal scene – whether it is the scene which the patient recognises as such, or whether it is the one whose recollection effects the cure. In practice these criteria are mingled together.

Analysis is likely to do harm. Because although one may discover in the course of it various things about oneself, one must have a very strong and keen and persistent criticism in order to recognise and see through the mythology that is offered or imposed on one. There is an inducement to say, 'Yes, of course, it must be like that'. A powerful mythology.

SOURCE: Ludwig Wittgenstein, *Lectures and Conversations* (1966).

LIONEL TRILLING

Freud's Last Book (1949)

IN July of 1938, during his London exile and in the painful last year of his long life, Sigmund Freud set down, in what we now know to be his ultimate formulation, the principles of the science he had created. He did not bring the brief work to an actual conclusion, but its translator is surely right in saying that it cannot be far from its planned end. As we have it, *An Outline of Psychoanalysis* consists of a remarkably clear statement of the psychoanalytical conception of the mind, a succinct explanation of neurosis, and a modest account of the analytical therapy. It breaks off at a point where Freud seems about to engage in moral consideration and cultural generalization.

The little book must be read in the light of its declared intention. It does not undertake to make a contribution of new ideas to psychoanalysis. Nor do its title and its lucid brevity constitute it a primer of the subject. It is not a difficult book, but neither is it elementary; and, as Freud says, it does not intend 'to compel belief or to establish conviction'. Its aim is simply 'to bring together the doctrines of psychoanalysis and to state them, as it were, dogmatically – and in the most concise form and in the most positive terms'.

An Outline of Psychoanalysis is to be read, then, as a sort of intellectual last testament of its author. Read so, it can serve as the occasion of a great intellectual, moral and even esthetic experience.

What strikes us first in the *Outline* is the style of Freud. Not the literary style merely, though that of course is remarkable, but the whole personal style – the 'life-style' of which the literary manner is but one expression.

Our culture inclines to prefer the bland and apologetic intellectual personality and we are set at ease by the self-depreciatory gesture. A kind of corrupt version of the scientific attitude serves to rationalize our wish to believe that one idea is as good as the next, and we like to suppose that a man is wrong in the degree that he is positive. And Freud is always positive – he startles us by seeming to speak as if he had put himself to school to Nature herself and had actually learned something in her fierce seminar.

This is the sign of his intellectual tradition. He liked to insist on his connection with the great pioneering natural scientists of the centuries before our own. Goethe was his acknowledged master and Diderot a kindred spirit, and he shared with these men not only their complex, organic view of the mind but also their vital confidence that mind and Nature could come to some large mutual understanding.

But Freud's positiveness, his belief that truth could actually be found, is also the sign of something particular in his temperament, particular in his vision of the world. It is an aspect of the passion of his response to the pain of life, the mark of his moral urgency, of his deep therapeutic commitment to the human cause.

And this, among other things, makes Freud pre-eminent among the modern theorists of the mind. The antagonists and modifiers of Freud's ideas may be compared among themselves as more or less cogent, but none of them can represent as adequately as Freud the stress and pain of the soul. It is charged against Freud by his opponents that he devaluates human life, that he does not sufficiently respect culture, or art, or love, or women, or the hope of human progress. Yet of those who make the accusation none has yet equalled Freud in actual respect for mankind by equalling him in the full estimation of human suffering or of the forces that cause it.

If we look for an analogue to Freud's vision of life, we find it, I think, in certain great literary minds. Say what we will about Freud's dealings with Shakespeare, his is the Shakespearian vision. And it is not mere accident that he levied upon Sophocles for the name of one of his central concepts.

No doubt the thing we respond to in great tragedy is the implication of some meaningful relation between free will and necessity, and it is what we respond to in Freud. One of the common objections to Freud is that he grants too much to necessity, and that, in doing so, he limits the scope of man's possible development. There is irony in the accusation, in view of the whole intention of psychoanalysis, which is to free the soul from bondage to the necessities that do not actually exist so that it may effectually confront those that do exist. Like any tragic poet, like any true moralist, Freud took it as one of his tasks to define the borders of necessity in order to establish the realm of freedom.

An Outline of Psychoanalysis makes abundantly clear how much account of necessity – of what the poet calls fate – Freud does take. He sees man as conditioned and limited by his own nature – by his biological heritage (in the *id*), by his long cultural history (in the *super-ego*). He believes that man in society will always be subject to more or less painful tensions, that what we call neurosis is only a quantitative variation in these tensions, the result of ascertainable causes. Man as Freud conceives him makes his own limiting necessity by being man.

This stern but never hopeless knowledge is precisely the vision of reality that we respond to in tragic art. Freud, when he spoke of the 'reality principle', set it in opposition to the 'pleasure principle', but the reality principle has its own charge of pleasure, perhaps even in the life of morality, certainly in the life of intellect and art. That is why I have spoken of *An Outline of Psychoanalysis* as being the occasion of an aesthetic experience.

One can respond to Freud with pleasure even when his drive to reality yields unacceptable results. For example, the *Outline* establishes as part of Freud's system an earlier idea of his that was once no more than speculative – it gives to the 'death instinct' a place equal in importance to that of the libidinal or creative instinct. The death instinct is a concept rejected by many of even the most thoroughgoing Freudian analysts (as Freud mildly notes); the late Otto Fenichel in his authoritative work on the neurosis argues cogently against it. Yet even if we should be led to reject the theory, we still cannot miss its grandeur, its ultimate tragic courage in acquiescence to fate.

The tragic vision requires the full awareness of the limits which necessity imposes. But it deteriorates if it does not match this awareness with an idea of freedom. Freud undertook to provide such an idea – it was his life work. And if in *An Outline of Psychoanalysis* he insists on the limiting conditions of man's biological and social heritage, yet one of the last sentences of the book is an instigation to the mastery of the hard inheritance. It is a sentence from Goethe: 'What you have inherited from your fathers, truly possess it so as to make it your very own.

SOURCE: Lionel Trilling, *A Gathering of Fugitives* (1949).

JOHN WISDOM

Philosophy, Metaphysics, and Psychoanalysis: Extract (1953)

THE evil effect of the cramping idea that every surprising, revealing, statement must be justified either by giving information which the person surprised lacks or by taking him through a process of strict deduction which he has been incapable of carrying out is not so easily detected in our judgement of what psychoanalysts say. This is because *part* of the justification for the things psychoanalysts say which surprise us *does* lie in information which most of us have not possessed. A metaphysician never tells us anything we haven't heard before. But psychoanalysts do. As Freud says: 'Errors and dreams are phenomena which were familiar to you. . . . The manifestations of neurosis, however, are an unknown region to you.' And though Freud works very much by recalling and connecting things familiar to us he also tells us astonishing stories. For example, he tells us of an experiment carried out by Bernheim.

> A man was placed in a condition of somnambulism, and then made to go through all sorts of hallucinatory experiences. On being awakened he seemed at first to know nothing at all of what had taken place during his hypnotic sleep. Berheim then asked him in so many words to tell him what had happened while he was under hypnosis. The man declared that he could not remember anything. Bernheim, however, insisted upon it, pressed him and assured him that he did know and that he must remember, and lo and behold! the man wavered, began to reflect, and remembered in a shadowy fashion first one of the occurrences which had been suggested to him, then something else, his recollection growing increasingly clear and complete until finally it was brought to light without a single gap.[1]

Then there is Morton Prince's story of the girl who while with her mouth she denied any memories connected with towers and the ringing of bells wrote with her hand an account of an experience which linked them with the grief and dread she had felt long ago when her mother was dangerously ill. In these cases it is new facts which make us say: 'Really all that had happened was still in his mind though at first he couldn't find it.' 'Really she remembered although she seemed not to do so.' 'In the depths, in the unconscious was grief though on the surface there was only a ridiculous fear.' So does it come about that new facts give us a new apprehension of old ones and a new apprehension of old facts new freedom in looking for new ones. The metaphysician doesn't even remind us of things we had forgotten. The psychoanalyst may. All this is well known and well recognised. Indeed the idea that the psychoanalyst holds minds in a fire which makes stand out what is written there in invisible ink has only too powerful a hold upon us. What is not well recognised is how much the psychoanalyst reveals things to us in the way Mr P, the philosopher, revealed to Mr A what he had before his eyes without realising it. Mr P, in order to reveal what he did to Mr A, modified and sophisticated Mr A's conception of a map. Doctors narrow and widen the use of old names for disorders in order to present better their connections and disconnections, partly because of new discoveries but partly also because of an increased grasp of the welter of detail with which they are dealing. Psycho-analysts in order to reveal to us things about ourselves modify and sophisticate our conceptions of love, hate, jealousy, envy, sympathy, sense of responsibility. They use familiar words not with a disregard of established usage but not in bondage to it.

Such procedure is always open to misunderstanding. Because of the element of diagnosis, prognosis, prediction, in psychoanalytic interpretations and generalisations it is not inappropriate to look for support for them in the way of new facts from investigation. But in so far as there is an unconventional element in the use of the words in which these interpretations are expressed no investigation will provide a proof of them on utterly conventional lines. The consequence is that people half feel that astonishing as is the new material psycho-analysts bring forward and impressive as is their reassembling of old material they still never 'quite prove' what they say.

They are right in a sense. The psychoanalysts' statements in so far as they are not expressed in strict accord with convention will never be proved in strict accord with convention. But this does not make them like statements which could be proved and are not. The psychoanalysts' statements will not be proved because they could not be. In so far as psychoanalysts' statements are conventionally expressed and precarious because they predict, they may be, in fact, unproved but they are not incapable of proof. On the contrary, in so far as they are conventionally expressed, they are capable of proof or disproof as any other prognosis, prophecy, prediction. It is only in so far as they are unconventionally expressed that they are incapable of conventional proof or disproof. But this doesn't leave them dubious, precarious, uncertain, or insusceptible of rational procedure. It means only that in so far as they are paradoxes they are paradoxical.

All this doesn't prove that psychoanalysts do prove what they say. Whether or no they do prove what they say in the manner appropriate to it is to be settled by considering with them what they draw attention to in justification of it – only this considering need not be a matter of coming upon something we have never come upon nor a matter of assembling what we have already come upon into a perfectly *conventional* proof.

Last time we reflected upon the peculiar character of the proof of paradox and upon how an unconscious tendency to avoid recognising this dangerous type of thought may make us miss what it can give us, and of how in particular this tendency can distort an understanding of the paradoxes of metaphysics and psychoanalysis.

And now someone may protest saying, 'But surely no one does reject what psychoanalysts say merely because they do not always use words quite literally. Surely we all recognise an elasticity in the use of words or in your grand phrase 'understand the logic of paradox', and surely we are prepared to apply this understanding.'.

I answer, 'Certainly we all recognise in some degree that language may be used paradoxically. And I do not claim that anyone rejects psychoanalytic claims merely because he does not recognise the power of paradox to reveal the truth or does not recognise it when considering what psychoanalysts say. But I do claim that in general we do not adequately recognise how often and how usefully people speak paradoxically, and I do claim that in particular our failure to recognise this adequately may contribute towards a person's rejecting psychoanalytic theories and psychoanalytic interpretations. I do claim that a person may use the paradoxical character of psychoanalytic statements in order to continue to reject them whatever evidence is assembled in support of them, and also in order to evade them by giving them a bogus acceptance.'

As to this bogus acceptance. It is not confined to psychoanalytic paradoxes. When someone says something astonishing, for example, 'St Augustine wasn't a saint', 'We're all mad really', 'Really we know nothing of the minds of others', 'Chairs and tables aren't really solid', we may at first expect him to produce in support of his statements facts unknown to the rest of us. When it turns out that he is not relying on facts not commonly known or only partly relying on these while it is also clear that no familiar facts could be conventionally described by his words, we may say, 'Ah I see you are using words in a special way of your own'; and when we say this we may no longer resist what is said and at the same time cease to pay much attention to it.

For example, when some metaphysical philosophers said, 'Metaphysical questions are meaningless', some people took this paradox literally and opposed it vigorously. But others said, 'Ah I see you are using the word 'meaningful' in an extraordinary way of your own. If you mean by 'a meaningful question' one that is either scientific or mathematical then of course metaphysical questions aren't meaningful'. And saying this they missed the point of paradox. They aimed to castrate it, and did – as far as they were concerned. In the same way when Freud said of things which would not ordinarily have been called sexual that they are, some people opposed this, but others cried 'Peace, peace' when there was no peace. For they said, 'No doubt he is using 'sexual' in a special sense of his own'.[2]

The consequence is that though it is true it is extremely dangerous to say that philosophers and psychoanalysts are not speaking literally. It is even dangerous to say that their paradoxes are paradoxes. For only in the shock of taking a paradox literally will people give that attention to concrete detail which will enable them to break old habits of grouping and recognise not merely *that* an old classification blinds and distorts but *how* it does.

Even when the logical character of paradoxical statements is fairly recognised and it is realised that in dealing with them critical attention must not become unsympathetic *nor* sympathetic attention uncritical, the metaphysical philosopher and the psychoanalytic philosopher still have big difficulties to meet.

In the first place, the material they have to deal with is subtle patterns in time, which are hard to grasp. The characters of questions are a matter of the parts they play in discussions – not only in actual discussions but in discussions which might have been carried on. The characters of persons are a matter of the parts they play in life – not only the parts they actually play but the parts they might have played had things been different. Lives and discussions are patterns in time and cannot be covered by the eye at a glance. Consequently without recalling innumerable incidents, without selecting significant items and assembling them like a dramatist, one cannot grasp these patterns.

In order to grasp complex and unmanageable patterns we are always using models, other patterns which we have grasped. With every name we apply we compare one thing with another, with many others. For example, we do this when we speak of a *current* of electricity. But of course we don't always set out explicitly those things with which we compare the complex reality we now have to grasp. The comparisons we make are at once valuable and dangerous. Without them we cannot bring order into bewildering flux but with them we may in the interests of unity blind ourselves to the diversity of the individual.

The metaphysician brings into the light certain old-established and invaluable models which we use in order to grasp the characters of sorts of questions, statements, proofs. He does this not because he plans to discard these models as merely misleading but so that we may control them instead of their controlling us, so that we may see how they illuminate and how they distort. We saw how the model of a hidden stream has defects as a model for consciousness. It leaves us wondering when and where the stream pushes the bodily machinery and how we ever came to know of the presence of this stream. But we saw too how the model of electricity or energy also has defects. It obscures the fact that it makes sense to talk of a person answering questions about how he feels according to how he feels in a way in which it makes no sense to talk of another person, B, answering questions about how A feels according to how he, B, feels. The old model, whatever its defects, does not obscure this. It misrepresents the peculiar right a person has to make statements about what is in his mind, for it represents it as like that of man who tells of the content of a room to which he alone has the key. But at least it does not ignore this peculiar right. Nor does it ignore the fact that a person can know the sensations and feelings of another only in so far as he himself has had sensations and feelings of a like sort – a man, a god, who had never felt pain could not know that another was in pain, only that he groaned. No wonder we resist the attempt to substitute for a model which recognises these things one which does not. The old one has served us well and will continue to do so; nor need we fear it once it no longer so fascinates us that we cannot recognise the differences between the model and that to which we apply it. But the fact remains that while this model has a monopoly in our minds it does on occasion lead us no end of a dance.

The psycho-analyst also tries to bring into the light models which dominate our thought, our talk, our feelings, our actions, in short our lives. And of course it is not the professional psychoanalyst only who does this – anyone who reflects upon people and tries to come at the truth does in some degree the same thing. Recently M. Blum broadcast some reflections on marriage and he then said again what we know has often been said, namely, that a woman in love tends to see her lover not as himself but as a prince charming. We might add, what also has often been said, that a man in love tends to see the woman with whom he is in love as a princess, a queen, an angel, a goddess. And we might add, what has less often been said, that a lover tends to see the person loved not only as a being with more than human, with divine, power, understanding, generosity, charm and unchanging love, but also as a being with demonic, Circe-like, wolf-like power, ruthlessness, and deceitfulness. We might say of someone, 'He sees Eve – you remember Eve Brown? – well believe it or believe it not, he sees her as a mysterious, not to say curious, combination of the Madonna of the Rocks and the Venus of the Venusberg.' Or again we might say, 'Deep down he sees every woman as a Cressida'.

When we try to bring out how someone sees something, say a goose, by saying that he sees it as something else, for example a swan, we may be concerned only to give an illuminating, co-ordinating, description of how he sees it, but we may also be concerned to give at the same time an explanation of why he sees it as he does. For example it is sometimes said of someone, 'He regards so and so as God Almighty', and this might be said even when the person in question had never heard of God. In that case, however, although what we say might be an illuminating description of him, it would give no explanation of why he regarded so and so with such reverence. On the other hand, if

F.—4*

the person of whom we speak had heard of God and believed in Him
and then perhaps lost that belief, we might say, 'He sees so and so as
God Almighty' and with these words give not merely a description
but part of the explanation of his attitude to so and so. The psychoanalyst tries to describe the present in terms which do not merely
connect the present with the present but also connect the present with
the past. For example, suppose we say, 'Jack regards every woman as
a Cressida'. This won't satisfy the psychoanalyst. What we have said
is well enough as a description. But it explains nothing. *Why* does
Jack regard every woman as a Cressida? He was never himself deceived
by Cressida. Nor by anyone like her. But is this last true? For hasn't
he known a woman who gave him all the love and all the good in all
the world he knew and then too often suddenly withdrew it and gave
that love and good to another? He has – in his mother's arms. No wonder that even when the lips of Venus are those of the Madonna they
still smile like the Mona Lisa.

The psychoanalyst seeks to bring into the light those models from
the past which for good and evil so powerfully influence our lives in
the present, so powerfully distort reality and so powerfully illuminate
it. For, of course, these models don't only distort. By no means.
No doubt the lover sees what we see isn't there. But doesn't he
also see what we can't see? Unquestionably Miss E. Brown is not
Aphrodite nor Diana. But then maybe she isn't the Miss Brown
we think we know. Hate may blind, but hate, even neurotic hate,
also reveals. The subtle evidence assembled to prove suspicions of
Albertine may not prove precisely those suspicions but they don't
prove nothing.[3]

The phantasies and models, illuminating but distorting, which
metaphysical philosophers and psychoanalysts try to bring to light
are unconscious. This makes the work of bringing them to light
difficult in a way intimately bound up with a difficulty we have already
looked at, the difficulty which lies in the proof of statements in which
the ordinary usage of words is followed and yet left behind, in which
words are used so that we cannot say that they are not being used in
their old sense nor yet that they are. Asked of such statements as these,
whether they are true or false, we are obliged to say, 'Well they are
and they aren't'.[4] And those situations in which we say of someone
that he unconsciously thinks this, imagines that, unconsciously wishes

this, feels that, are always ones in which, when asked whether he thinks this, imagines that, wishes this, feels that, we are inclined to say, 'Well he does and he doesn't'. No wonder the logic of paradox is important to the understanding of statements of the sort 'Unconsciously he . . .'.

Take now the statement, 'Unconsciously we think of the soul as a hidden stream, as a little bird within'. Someone may protest, 'What nonsense. Primitive people may have had this idea but we are aware that consciousness or the mind or the soul is not a material thing at all, however transparent or elusive'.

It is true that we do not watch for the soul leaving the body in sleep or at death or cut open skulls extremely quickly in order to catch a glimpse of the soul. Further, for ascertaining the truth about birds and clouds we count Jack as good as his neighbour while for ascertaining the truth about a soul we count Jack better, if the soul is his.

Nevertheless, it is also true that we seldom consciously and in so many words recognise the difference between souls and minds on the one hand and on the other hand ghosts, winds, clouds and streams. And even people who pay lip service to this difference may not recognise the difference between this difference and the difference between stone, ice and water. We sometimes ask, 'How, when and where does the soul act upon the body?' We sometimes say, 'The most careful physiologist cannot find thoughts or feelings, the mind or the soul', and say it either with ill-concealed satisfaction at there being still something which eludes the scientist or with an equally inappropriate innuendo that to believe in mind or the soul is unscientific. In these ways we betray the feebleness of our grasp of the idiosyncrasy of the logic of the soul, that is of the way questions about the soul are settled. We betray this again when we are perplexed by a sceptical person who suddenly, by reasoning which every feature of our language seems to condone, forces us towards a formula of doubt which seems to express the metaphysical confirmation of our worst fears. We are at once dominated by the model of the stream, the bird, the manikin, the ghost and yet unconscious of it.

Someone may protest, 'I see that while there are features of our thought about the soul which are in favour of saying that we are not dominated by the model of the bird and the stream, there are also features of it which are in favour of saying that we are. But why say that we are unconscious of this model? We talk openly enough of the stream of consciousness.'

It is true that we talk openly of the stream of consciousness, of the stream of thoughts and feelings, and even of the mysterious inhabitant that in sleep may leave the body and visit again places it used to know. But if a metaphysician says, 'The soul you know is not a bird nor a stream nor even a wind', then we are apt to reply, 'Well, of course. We know the soul isn't a bird or a stream or a wind. Primitive people may have thought so but we are aware that the soul is not a material thing at all, however elusive or transparent.' And with these words we may, while admitting that the myth of the bird lingers in our language and even in a sense in our thought, avoid recognising its power, its power to lead us a purely metaphysical dance and even to bewilder us in factual inquiries by mixing with the difficulties of getting the facts a feeling of mystery which comes from metaphysical misunderstanding. For example, when the question is asked, 'Do animals, do dogs, think?', the inquiry is sometimes bedevilled by mixing with the difficulty of finding out what dogs are capable of, a difficulty which is expressed by saying, 'We can only find out how dogs *behave*. We can't know anything about their minds or indeed whether they have any'. This last doubt is nothing but a special case of 'No one can know anything about the mind of another, only about how he behaves'. Again, Mr Bernal in a discussion about science and ethics which was carried on in *Nature* accuses Mr Waddington of believing in dubious and elusive entities such as the super-ego. And this accusation though it arises only in part from metaphysical misunderstanding of the logic of mental events does arise in part from this and in part from another metaphysical misunderstanding which comes from thinking of the mind, the soul, the super-ego, as something not only behind bodily events but also behind mental events. And people are suspicious of the unconscious and of unconscious mental events not only because they misunderstand the logic of paradox but also because they think of unconscious mental events as behind, below, deeper down than, the conscious ones as there are deeper and deeper depths in a stream. The two misunderstandings encourage each other. We are at once dominated by the model of the stream and the ghost, and yet unconscious of its power.

It is the same with the models the power of which the psychoanalyst tries to bring home to us. He says, perhaps, 'In your feelings your parents are inside you, watching every act you do, cognizant of every thought you think, and consequently hurt, pleased, angered not only by what you do but also by what you think of doing', or 'Unconsciously you think your parents are inside you'. We say, perhaps, 'What nonsense' or 'If you mean that I hear from time to time what used to be called the voice of conscience, why don't you say so instead of talking in this ridiculous new way'.

Just as the metaphysician must assemble evidences in support of his claim that we not only speak as if the soul were a hidden manikin but from time to time think and feel as if this were so, the psychoanalyst must wait until the person to whom he speaks provides the evidences which show how inadequate is the expression, 'You hear from time to time the voice of conscience', to cover the facts he refers to by the words, 'You have always the idea that your parents are within you'.

In thinking of the metaphysician and the psychoanalyst as trying to bring to light unconscious models we come again upon what I have called bogus acceptance, but now of a rather different sort. For example, the metaphysician says perhaps, 'You have the idea that language is an exact calculus'. Someone may reply, 'I know, I know. Words are vague and we don't sufficiently recognize this'. What is one to say then? And yet the person who says this may have an utterly inadequate idea of how insufficiently we recognise the vagueness of language.[5] A moment later he may be found treating a question which because of the vagueness of language has no definite answer as if it had one, or insisting that it is a different question, one which has a definite answer, or insisting because it hasn't a definite answer that it isn't a question.

In a like way someone may say to a psychoanalyst, 'Yes I know it has been discovered that many men secretly envy women their role in life' or even, 'I know I secretly envy women their role in life', while having the feeblest apprehension of the concrete detail which backs these statements. The envy itself makes it the harder to accept the humiliation of recognising it. A man may say, 'All right, all right, I know that old stuff about seeing the woman I am in love with as my mother', and still not be alive to the ramifications of the power of that model from the past which illuminates and distorts the present.

Besides all these ways in which the procedure, the difficulties, and the aims, of psychoanalysis are reflected in metaphysics, there is another connection, so I believe, which brings them closer still. As I have said, I believe that metaphysics arises from applying, in a peculiarly profound study of what gives us the right to make statements of this type or that, models which are inappropriate. In particular the deductive model is appropriate only in a non-profound study of what gives one a right to make this or that statement of a given type. While we are concerned only with what gives a person a right to make a particular statement of a certain type – ethical, mathematical, physical, psychological – and are prepared to admit as giving him a right to make that statement other statements of *the same type* the inductive-deductive models described in books on logic are adequate. But sometimes we are concerned to push further the inquiry as to what gives him a right to make the statement he does. Then when he submits premises which consist of statements of the same type we ask him what right he has to accept those premises. At once the inductive-deductive models are no longer adequate. For only statements of the same type are connected on the inductive-deductive models. Consequently if we are dissatisfied with premises which are of the same type as a certain statement and yet insist that only what is connected with a statement inductively or deductively really gives a right to make that statement we are bound to conclude that in the end no one really has any right to make that statement or any other of the type in question. There is, therefore, logical confusion and logical penetration at the back of metaphysics.

But if we now ask, 'What drives people to pursue to such lengths questions of the sort?' 'Do we know this?', 'What right have we to make these statements?', and what preserves the power of those models which keep us for ever seeking but never finding the knowledge we seem to want, then it occurs to us to wonder whether the forces at work in this curiously unsatisfactory struggle, which never ends in success or in failure, aren't in part the same as those at work in those other struggles in which something is for ever sought and never found, struggles which, in their turn, are connected with an earlier time when there was something, namely the world of the grown-ups, knowledge of which we desperately desired and equally desperately dreaded.

When we consider the obstinate doubts of the metaphysician, 'Can one ever know what's right or wrong?', 'Can one ever know what others think or feel?', they readily remind us of the chronic doubts of the neurotic and the psychotic: 'Have I committed the unpardonable sin?'; 'Aren't they all against me really?' On the road to Solipsism – which is the doctrine not that I matter to nobody but that nobody exists but me – on the road to Solipsism, there blows the same wind of loneliness which blows on the road to the house with walls of glass which none can break. In the labyrinth of metaphysics are the same whispers as one hears when climbing Kafka's staircases to the tribunal which is always one floor further up. Is it perhaps because of this that when in metaphysics we seem to have arranged by a new technique a new dawn, then we find ourselves again on Chirico's sad terraces, where those whom we can never know still sit and it is neither night nor day?

We may hurry away and drown the cries that follow from those silent places – drown them in endless talk, drown them in the whine of the saxophone or the roar from the stands. Or, more effective, we may quiet those phantasmal voices by doing something for people real and alive. But if we can't we must return, force the accusers to speak up, and insist on recognising the featureless faces. We can hardly do this by ourselves. But there are those who will go with us and, however terrifying the way, not desert us.

SOURCE: John Wisdom, *Philosophy and Psychoanalysis* (1953).

NOTES

1. *Introductory Lectures on Psycho-Analysis*, p. 85.
2. Ibid. Lecture XX, 'The Sexual Life of Man'.
3. Consider also William Sansom's *The Body*.
4. It is sometimes said that the unconscious knows nothing of logic and even that it is not bound by logic. But this is a mystery-making way of talking. The unconscious knows as much as any one else about logic. And the laws of logic can no more break down in the world of the unconscious than they can in any other world. What is true is that, in any sphere whatever, to connect our statements in accordance with the laws of logic serves us well only in so far as the language in which we make those statements is applicable to the phenomena with which we are dealing without distorting those phenomena in those respects with which we are concerned. There are no doubts that some cows are more like horses than others, but upon the whole the animals which we actually come across fall very definitely under one or other of the animal names in our vocabulary and the law 'If it's a cow it can't be a horse' serves us well. But if Nature were to begin to produce beasts as much like cows as horses, as much like dogs as cats, our language would begin to

break down again and again and the law 'If it's a cow it can't be a horse', though it would not become false, would become as much a menace as a help.

Now in describing people, though our language serves us well enough up to a point, we are often concerned with likenesses and differences which it not only fails to reveal but, in so far as we rely upon, it conceals. Consequently for any minute understanding of people's spiritual states laws such as 'If he loves he doesn't hate', 'He can't think this and also not think it' become as much a menace as a help.

5. Compare Karen Horney in *New Ways in Psycho-Analysis* (New York, 1939) on the meaning of the word 'unconscious'.

IAGO GALDSTON

Freud and Romantic Medicine (1956)

THIS essay is offered as a contribution to the exegesis of psychoanalysis. It aims to lay bare some of the sources of Freud's ideas, and to specifically relate them to certain relevant ideas promulgated in Romantic Medicine.

I approach my task in the dual role of psychiatrist and medical historian. Both disciplines are requisite, psychiatry in order to understand Freud's own *élan vital*, and medical history to adequately appreciate the cultural setting and intellectual climate in which Freud grew up, matured, and effected his revolution in psychiatry.

Mine is not the first attempt to trace Freud's ideas to their sources of origin. Indeed there is a welter of such attempts. Many of them are concerned with uncovering so-called forerunners to, and anticipators of, Freud. But there also have been some more meritorious attempts, such as were made by Dr and Mrs Bernfeld, Marie Dorer of Darmstadt, and Louise von Karpinska of Poland. The most competent and the most penetrating efforts in this direction, however, stand to the credit of Fritz Wittels. His biographic study of Freud, together with his *Freud and His Time*, afford one valuable insight into the personality of Freud and into the relatedness of his ideas to those of his forerunners.

My own efforts at 'tracing' Freud's ideas to their sources of origin are favored above those of my predecessors, including Wittels, in that I have, as they had not, access to the Fliess letters, and to the data concerning Freud's childhood, and young manhood given in the Jones biography. Of the two the Fliess letters are the more important.

In the exegesis of psychoanalysis three factors call for thorough study: first and foremost the person of Freud; second, the derivation and structuralization of his ideas; and third, the impact of those ideas upon the realm of science and thought. This is patently a task of gigantic dimensions, and at this juncture I can pretend to no more than a modest enterprise.

What is to be noted relative to the person of Freud? Freud was a Jew living in anti-Semitic surroundings. One of his earliest memories of his father revolved about an episode in which the father was insulted and could not, or would not, avenge himself, but swallowed the insult in a manner that seemed craven to Freud.

Freud was poor. He grew up in a home where want was not de-praving but where it was an indwelling and abiding *Sorge*. Freud knew and suffered the hobbling effects of poverty for the greater portion of his childhood, his youth, and young manhood.

Freud grown into manhood was compelled by want to do that which promised him a living rather than what he wanted or would have preferred to do. His entire being was conditioned by these cruel and degrading determinants. The poverty that engulfed Freud was not simply economic: it was all-pervading, it was atmospheric. It is diffi-cult to conceive the qualitative character of the poverty that engulfed a poor Jew living in Vienna during the latter half of the last century. It was not so much depraving in its effects as it was overwhelming and paralysing. In such an atmosphere only those survive who have great endurance, and only those prevail who are gifted with an in-ordinate drive and with such competences as can lift them over the barriers of social insignificance, economic want, and racial prej-udice.

Fortunately Freud was endowed with just such gifts and competences. He had an inordinate drive, great energy, and a superb intellect. But it must be understood that Freud's historical position is essentially the resultant of the interplay between his native qualities and the depriva-tional and provocative setting in which they operated. It is both con-ceivable and highly probable that had Freud not been subjected to the goadings of his manifold poverty he would not have risen beyond the relative mediocrity of an able man. Again, were Freud less gifted he would most likely have been lost in that anonymity of the *Klein-burgertum* or the *Handelsstand* that embraced in its amorphous ambient the greater portion of Vienna's Jewry. But Freud was ambitious. That more than anything else is the outstanding characteristic of his personality. He was ambitious to avenge the Stygian nothingness of his origin, to more than make up for the insignificance of his patrimony and the devastating mediocrity, the undistinguished platitudinousness of the world in which he suffered his youth.

Given his goading resentment, his driving ambition, and his gifts, it can be predicated that Freud would have succeeded in any undertaking. He would have made his mark in any field. Whether it would have been so great a mark, so shining an achievement as that represented by psychoanalysis, is a moot question. For in the fruition of psycho-analysis are implicated certain fortuitous circumstances extraneous to Freud and his immediacies. Chief among these fortuitous and extraneous circumstances were the then prevailing convictions and patterns of scientific thought. And equally fortuitous and fortunate were the circumstances that brought Freud in contact with, and exposed him to, the influences and inspirations of a number of men – Breuer, Charcot, and Fliess. The last named, in my judgement, had the profoundest effect upon Freud's intellectual development – vastly greater than any of Freud's biographers have recognised or acknowledged.[1]

Fliess has received but scant justice from Freud's biographers. Of course, Freud was their main concern and Fliess was but a side issue. In the Fliess letters, ingenuously labelled *Aus den Anfängen der Psychoanalyse*,[2] (and not Freud's letters to Fliess) they sought for and found Freud, not Fliess. Of Fliess they were content to note that 'he was said to be' charming and that he was some sort of crank about numbers. That and a few derogatory opinions quoted from among his disagreeing contemporaries and the picture is complete![3] Fliess was not of Freud's stature, but he is treated by the Freudians as Freud was initially treated by his own uninformed contemporaries. From this general indictment I must exempt Fritz Wittels. Of Fliess he wrote: '[er] ist ein geistreicher und spekulativer Kopf, in mehr als einer Hinsicht Freud verwandt.'[4]

I will return to Fliess later. For the present I want to revert to Freud's driving ambition to be pre-eminent – little matter in what – so but he be pre-eminent.[5]

Freud was lapped in the myth of the hero. There is the apocryphal tale of his birth with a cowl, and the soothsayer's, in this case an old woman's prediction that he would rise in the world and become a chancelor. Freud himself nurtured the aspirations of an heroic destiny. Long before he had any claim to distinction, Freud wrote seriously concerning his future biographers, and how difficult he was making it for them by destroying all materials bearing upon his intimate life.

Twice in his life he expunged his past. The first time in 1885, and the last in 1907. On two occasions he completely destroyed all his correspondence, notes, diaries and manuscripts.[6] Writing to his betrothed in 1885 – Freud was then 29 years of age – he reported the destruction of his private papers, and observed:

> I cannot leave here and cannot die before ridding myself of the disturbing thought of who might come by the old papers. . . . Let the biographers chafe; we won't make it too easy for them. Let each one of them believe he is right in his 'conception of the development of the Hero': Even now I enjoy the thought of how they will all go astray.[7]

It is interesting to speculate why Freud was so eager to blot out the past.

There can be little doubt that Freud felt himself heroically predestined and convinced that it was up to him to eventuate this heroic destiny. For that Freud lacked neither energy nor enterprise. Describing Freud's three hospital years – 1884–7 – Jones writes: 'Freud was constantly occupied with the endeavor to make a name for himself by discovering something important in either clinical or pathological medicine.'[8] Jones ascribes this drive to Freud's eagerness to marry 'a year or two earlier.' But this explanation is not convincing. The simple fact is that Freud was an ambitious man, even unto his old age, and it is quite consistent for an ambitious man to try to make a name for himself.

Before Freud turned to the treatment of nervous and mental diseases he ventured into a number of fields, seeking in each to make a name for himself. He experimented with pharmacological products, he worked in physiology, embryology, in neuroanatomy, dabbled in children's diseases, and tried his skill as a medical compiler, translator, and author. He was competent in each, came close to gaining distinction on several occasions, but attained in none the pre-eminence he sought and craved.[9]

That came to him only after he had laboured long in the treatment of nervous and mental diseases. And here we witness an instance of Freud's great good fortune, for at the beginning of this departure and for many years thereafter, Freud had for friend and mentor the gentle, generous, and ingenious Josef Breuer. The relationship between Breuer and Freud is too well known to require retelling, though it is worth noting that in later years Freud was privately hostile toward Breuer, though publicly he always spoke of Breuer in terms of praise and gratitude.[10]

Freud not infrequently referred to Breuer as the Founder of Psychoanalysis. This, as Jones observes, is an exaggeration. It was an overassessment of Breuer's share, and it is to be seriously doubted if Breuer ever accepted the reference gladly or as a compliment. For Breuer was not sympathetic to Freud's 'wild speculations'.[11] He was an orthodox scientist, an adherent of the school of Helmholtz, a devotee of Goethe and of Fechner. Yet there can be no doubt that by his participation in Breuer's famous case, Frl. Anna O., Freud was launched on a tangent of curiosity and interest which ultimately led him to the formulation of his theory and system of psychoanalysis. But Breuer disassociated himself from Freud long before the latter had gone far in these directions. And the reason for this was not as it is commonly alleged, that Breuer became alarmed when Frl. Anna attempted to involve him in some of her sexual fancies, but rather that Breuer could not accept Freud's speculations.

It is this and not specifically Freud's emphasis on the role of sexuality in hysteria that estranged Breuer. Yet the common opinion holds to the contrary and Breuer is made to appear a shy, timid, prudish old maid of a man. Sexuality in hysteria was a secondary factor at issue – the primary one was in the nature of a broad philosophical difference. Freud himself described it clearly in his 'Autobiographical Study'.[12] The issue between him and Breuer revolved around the problem 'when and how do mental processes become pathogenic'. Breuer advocated a physiological theory and Freud a psychological. Freud, in his own words, suspected at the root of the pathogenic mental processes the operation of 'intentions and purposes such as are to be observed in normal life'. It was the thwart and repression of such intentions and purposes that, according to Freud, proved pathogenic. If one but granted that premise, it was incontrovertible that in our society the intentions and purposes of sexuality were subject to the greatest thwart and repression. But the premise was *not* granted, either by Breuer or by the world of science. The premise denied, all that was derived therefrom was likewise denied and rejected. One man in

Freud's immediacy, however, did not reject the premise; that man, to Freud's great good fortune, appeared on the scene at just the right time, and that man was Wilhelm Fliess.

But before dealing with Fliess' role in Freud's intellectual development, it is imperative that we grasp in its full import what it was that Freud premised and why it was so grossly rejected and violently opposed. To state the issue bluntly and at its simplest – the imputation to life and to its manifold phenomena of intention and purpose was anathema to all the 'best brains' in biology and medicine. Intentions and purposes smacked of vitalism, and reeked of teleology. Life, according to prevailing scientific belief, was to be accounted for in terms of matter and energy, in terms of molecules in motion. Purpose and intention had neither place nor meaning in the realm of science. Yet Freud postulated not molecules and motion but intention and purpose – 'such,' he added, 'as are to be observed in normal life'. Is it not understandable then why Brücke, Meynert, and Breuer, those closest to Freud in his student years and during his early manhood, were alienated and aggrieved? Freud had in effect betrayed them. He had renounced their common faith. Brücke, Meynert, and Breuer belonged to the school of von Helmholtz, a school whose adherents, embracing the outstanding biologists, physiologists, and physicians of the time, were bitterly and aggressively opposed to every theory of biology that posited any factor other than matter and energy.

The most outspoken and belligerent representative of this school of thought was not von Helmholtz, but Emil du Bois-Reymond, the Prussian patriot of French extraction. Brücke was a close friend of du Bois-Reymond. Bernfeld cites a letter written by du Bois-Reymond which contains the following affirmation:

> Brücke and I pledged a solemn oath to put into effect this truth: 'No other forces than the common physical-chemical ones are active within the organism. In those cases which cannot at the time be explained by these forces one has either to find the specific way or form of their action by means of the physical-mathematical method or to assume new forces equal in dignity to the chemical-physical forces inherent in matter, reducible to the force of attraction and repulsion.'

'Intention and purpose' did not belong to that order of forces deemed equal in dignity to the physical-chemical forces. Hence,

Freud and his theories were not acceptable among the scientifically orthodox and respectable.

I have quoted Freud's own words on the differences between himself and Breuer, and underscored the words 'intention and purpose'. From this it might be assumed that in his own mind Freud was clear as to 'where he stood and what he intended'. But such an assumption would be grossly erroneous. Freud never made a clean break with the school of von Helmholtz, and I doubt that he ever, in the long span of his life, grasped the true issue that separated him from orthodox psychology. Freud was all his life, as Wittels named him, the Antiphilosopher, and 'the issue' was in the last analysis philosophical. Freud, to use modern terms, was an ethologist, and an ecological and holistic scientist, *malgré soi*.

Therein lies the wonder and the tragedy of his association with Fliess – a wonder in the effect it had upon his thinking and endeavors, and tragic in the tawdry *finis* that was writ to that friendship. Tragic, too, is the disparagement and calumny heaped upon Fliess' person and memory by the adulating partisans of Freud.

Who was Wilhelm Fliess? Little was known of him before the Fliess letters came to light, and even now there is but scant information about him as a personage. Those who have commented on him, in his relations to Freud, tend to belittle him. Jones is frequently and overtly abusive in his treatment of Fliess. Hence, we not only know little of Fliess but that little which is published is patently derogatory and prejudicial.

The Fliess letters are but half a story. We do not have those written by Fliess to Freud.[13] Freud destroyed them. Freud would have destroyed his own letters to Fliess, but fortunately they were saved. Unfortunately not all of them are published, nor are those published given in their entirety. Of 284 epistles only 168 have been made public. The explanation that some of the materials have been kept out because their publication would 'be inconsistent with professional or personal confidence', leaves one, me at least, unsatisfied and unhappy.

Knowing so very little about Fliess, how are we to gauge his influence upon Freud? The answer is – by internal evidence, that is by the evidence we can gain in a careful scrutiny of Fliess' own thoughts and writings.

Were we to take our cue from Jones and Ernst Kris, Fliess would be written off as a fantastic numerologist, an otherwise gracious, informed, and charming man, but still, one who somehow developed a mathematical monomania. Neither Kris nor Jones have attempted to gain insight into the derivation of this so-called mathematical monomania, nor have they related it to Fliess' other preoccupations, to bisexuality, to right- and left-handedness, to the nasal reflex, to the periodicity of fertility and infertility. Had they troubled to do so in the framework of the requisite historical understanding they could have discovered that collectively all this has meaning and that from this meaning Freud drew deep insight and much inspiration.

What is the commonality, the embracing persuasion of Fliess' endeavors? I am not certain that he ever expressed it as such – but it is unmistakably that of Romantic Medicine. For in Romantic Medicine one finds not only precisely those concerns which Fliess pursued but also the exact counterpart of his own and of Freud's orientation to Nature and to Man. This orientation Freud derived directly from Fliess during the fifteen years of their intimate relation. Freud was not a student of philosophy and there is no evidence to show that he came under the tutorial influence of any one else as schooled and biased in these directions as was Fliess.[14]

It is not possible to expound in this presentation the ample meaning and the historical as well as philosophical significance of Romantic Medicine. More nonsense has been written about Romantic Medicine, especially in the English language, than was ever contained in it. Yet, though indeed Romantic Medicine embraced much flimsy and brain-fevered speculations, its fundamental assumptions, derived from the *Naturphilosophie* of Schelling, were not only profoundly penetrating and wise, but are finding validation and support in present-day science and biology.[15]

Here I must content myself in merely highlighting the distinctions, the differences, the antipodal positions of Romantic Medicine, and the medicine so self-consciously triumphant in the days of Fliess and Freud. Recall the affirmations of du Bois-Reymond, who spoke not only for himself and for Brücke, but for the entire of the so-called school of von Helmholtz, that is for the whole of the modern world of science and biology. Du Bois wrote: 'No other forces than the common physical-chemical ones are active within the organism.' This affirmation, this pledge, made with the pugnacious overtones of a challenge – 'and woe to him who does not do likewise' was in effect but the reiteration of the pledged commitment of that science which came into being with the Age of Enlightenment. It was but the echo of the words and persuasions of Condorcet, of la Mettrie, of Holbach. These persuasions are tersely summed up by Ernst Cassirer in the following words: 'All the processes of nature, including those commonly called 'intellectual', the whole physical and moral order of things, are reducible to matter and motion and are completely explicable in terms of these two concepts.'[16] In the purview of la Mettrie, the human body is an immense clock constructed with much artifice. In Holbach's *Système de la Nature* it is stipulated that no aspect of nature is to be introduced into the philosophy of nature which is explicable only in terms of man and his appetites and desires. It is the structure of the atoms that forms man, and their motion that propels him forward; conditions not dependent on him determine his nature and direct his fate. In this philosophy of science there is neither place nor acceptance for 'intention and purpose', the two factors the misadventures of which are posited by Freud at the root of, as the *fons et origo* of, hysteria and the neuroses.

La Mettrie is usually assessed as an extremist among the philosophers of the Enlightenment, and that is correct. But in his postulates and premises he is in essential agreement with the leading philosophers of his age. The realm of philosophy, however, was not totally under their sway. There was also Leibnitz. And he stood athwart the philosophy of rationalistic materialism. Leibnitz was born in 1646 and died in 1716. Chronologically, therefore, he belongs to the seventeenth rather than to the eighteenth century. But the influence of Leibnitz's philosophy had the character of a delayed action. Its principal theatre of growth and operation was Germany and the Germanic countries, and the growth of German thought was guided by the influence of Leibnitz. The main trend of Leibnitz's thought gained recognition very slowly, but its penetration was nevertheless deep and effective.

What was the main trend of Leibnitz's thought? It can without distortion be summed up in one word 'appetency' which can in turn be translated as *desire, appetite, intention, purpose*. This stood in opposition to the rationalistic materialism of the French and English philosophies of the Enlightenment. Perhaps the terms 'athwart' and 'in opposition' do not correctly define the relation of Leibnitz's philosophy to that of the leading French school. For Leibnitz accepted, in the main, the Cartesian postulates of matter and motion. Where he departed from the Cartesian position, and this departure does in effect equate to an athwart position, amount to this – Leibnitz endowed 'matter' with 'entelechy'. Leibnitz's indivisible units of matter were named by him monads. There is a tendency current to equate them to the atom of present day physics. But the equation is not warranted. Leibnitz's monads were conceived of as units of matter possessed not only of the qualities of extension, impenetrability, gravity, etc., but also of desire, aversion, and memory.[17]

'The monads,' as Leibnitz envisaged them, 'are the subjects from which all events originate, and the principle of their activity, of their progressive development, is not the connection of causes and effects, but a teleological relationship.'[18] Teleology here implies purpose, inward form pressing for realization, and the specific, dynamic, process of becoming, as distinct from that of being.

The concept of inward form pressing for realization inspired a new feeling for nature and deeply influenced the intellectual history of Germany. Its finest form is witnessed in the *Naturphilosophie* that flourished during the latter part of the eighteenth and the first half of the nineteenth century.

The span between Leibnitz and Romantic Medicine is bridged by the philosophical contributions of Kant, Fichte, and Schelling. And Schelling was the Prince of the Romanticists. This may be given as the quintessence of the Romanticist's faith, a faith witnessed alike in *Naturphilosophie* and in Romantic Medicine, that the whole of the universe and that of being, human and all other, is bound together in an all-pervading, all-meaningful relatedness, and only in this relatedness is any portion of the total to be comprehended.[19] This does not premise a static relatedness, but rather one of continued becoming. The relatedness of being is in a sustained process of transition toward newer states of being. In the light of this it is understandable how the idea of evolution crystallised in the speculative thinking of the Romanticists. Goethe who must be counted a partisan of the Romanticists, wrote on the metamorphoses of plants, and Lorenz Oken in the last issue of *Isis* (1835)[20] a publication which he founded, sketched a theory on the evolution of man which was substantially validated in Darwin's great work.

I doubt that Fliess would have relished being counted among the

Romanticists. Yet it is a fact that in his preoccupations he stands in spiritual and intellectual kinship with the Romanticists. However, those who have treated of Fliess, notably the Freudian authors, would deny him even this much of recognition. They tend to write him off as a 'mathematical monomaniac' a deluded numerologist. The derogatory opinions of Aelby to the effect that Fliess 'was suffering from over-valuation of an idea' (a charge which could with greater warrant and in many more instances be levelled against Freud), Riebold's characterisation of Fliess as 'a player with numbers', and Frese's opinion that Fliess' nasal reflex neurosis 'verges on the mystical' are cited with seeming relish in patent endorsement.[21] It is not my intention to elaborate a defense of Fliess. But it is my intention to show how little those who are preoccupied with Fliess' so-called numerology understand what Fliess was attempting to establish. In the introduction to his major work *Der Ablauf des Lebens*[22] Fliess wrote:

> Very ancient is the question as to which laws determine the course of life. Manifold have been the answers. Belief and scientific notions have alternately ventured as solution. But be it a deity, be it the stars, be it cosmic forces that lie at the origin of the weather, be it finally the miracles of germination – in life, illness, and death they were ever *external* causes that influenced the living being in a so to say disturbing way. According to what pattern of inner-organization life, not only human, but all earthly life, takes its course, how through this inner organization the generations are linked, and how with no less certainty than the hour of birth is the hour of death predestined – this will be demonstrated in these pages for the first time and in a completely new way. Not through any hypotheses; but solely by means of the most exact, mathematical analysis.

It must be granted forthwith that his 'exact mathematical analysis' does not stand up under critical testing. But that does not invalidate his basic hypothesis that 'nicht äussere Ursachen' but rather some 'innere Ordnung' determine the evolvement and span of life. This is in effect a deep rooted conviction shared by all in the biological sciences. Nor is the possibility to be entirely precluded that some mathematical factor-formula may yet be derived which will prove statistically valid for the *hypothetical* individual.[23]

Fliess' egregious blunder lies in his attempt to postulate a formula precisely applicable to every and any given individual. But Fliess' preoccupation with a mathematical formula to express the *Ablauf des*

Lebens must be considered in conjunction with his other interests. Only thuswise can one appreciate his kinship with Romantic Medicine. Fliess was interested in bisexuality, in handedness, in sinistration and dextration, in the problem of mortality and death, in the periodicities of fertility and of sterility, in the relation of the nose to genitality. He anticipated what is currently termed the rhythm method of contraception. These items not only deeply concerned the partisan of Romantic Medicine but they were indeed at the very core of its dynamic philosophy. Lorenz Oken affirmed it as a cardinal principle – 'Erstens liegt allen Gestalten der Natur der Gedanke der Zahl zugrunde.'[24] Oken's primal figure was not an integer but rather zero. Rhythm and repetitiveness, the Myth of the Eternal Return, was an essential premise in the philosophy of Romantic Medicine. Novalis wrote: 'In so far as one envisages life as a complete whole, to that extent is it subject to division into periods and epochs. These periods and epochs of life must perforce bear a relationship to one another; for life must exhibit a *rhythmus* in its evolvement, and must express a harmony.[25] This thesis of periodicity is reflected in Fliess' mathematical calculations. Polarity, the relationship of apposites, was 'die eigentliche Lebenslehre der Romantik'.[26] This too is reflected in Fliess' theory of bisexuality. In the writings of J. J. Bachofen are to be found precise and specific references to *sinistration* and *dextration* and 'die höhere Würde der linken Seite' (the greater dignity of the left side), identical with the ideas propounded by Fliess: the left side belongs to the female, the right side to the male. 'In the morals and customs of civil and cultural life, in the peculiarities of attire and grooming, as also in folklore, and no less in the meaning of expressions, the same idea is repeatedly encountered, *major honos laevarum partium*, 'the greater dignity of the left side'.[27]

In citing these homologues to Fliess' theories, in Romantic Medicine, I have no intention to suggest that Fliess plagiarised the writings of his predecessors. I intend only to define the framework of his thinking and to highlight its kinship with *Naturphilosophie* and Romantic Medicine. Whatever his specific preoccupations, they were set within the matrix of the philosophy of the Romanticists, and from this matrix, through the long enthusiastic and friendly indoctrinations of Freud by Fliess, Freud derived and nurtured his original ideas, which, in time, and *by dint of other labors* yielded his philosophy and system of psychoanalysis.

In the Introduction to the volume of the Fliess letters there is a chapter entitled 'Psychoanalysis as an Independent Science'. This is a paradoxical affirmation, for it lies in the very nature of a science to *not be* independent, otherwise it cannot be a science but only a mysterium, an esoteric discipline. Yet the intention of the affirmation is transparent. It but reiterates Freud's own claims – that he, and he alone, created psychoanalysis. Historically that is not to be doubted or questioned. But to grasp the full implications of this affirmation one must scrutinise it deeply. It is true that Freud created psychoanalysis but the question remains 'out of what'. Completely original, that is, virginal creativity is vouchsafed only to the musical and mathematical geniuses. Those in the plastic and graphic arts may in some instances be granted this supreme gift of inventiveness. But no one who contributes to science can be 'virginally creative'. He can only apply his creative genius to such singular insights as may come to him in the perspective of antecedent knowledges. The independence of Freud, the *Unabhängigkeit* of psychoanalysis, is meaningful and understandable only in the light of the fact that Freud was an autodidact. Freud vigorously intended to be original. He consistently abstained (to the extent possible) from acquainting himself with what others had done or had thought before him. He wrote to Fliess, 'I do not want to read, because it stirs up too many thoughts and stints me of the satisfaction of discovery.'[28] Reading, he discovered that 'It is the oldest ideas which are the most useful, as I am belatedly finding out.'[29] In another letter he wrote: 'What have you got to say to the suggestion that the whole of my brand-new theory of the primary origins of hysteria is already familiar and has been published a hundred times over, through several centuries ago?'[30] Such discoveries disconcerted him. Freud preferred to think first and to 'study' later. When he was working on his Dream Interpretation he wrote to Fliess: 'First I want to get my own ideas into shape, then I shall make a thorough study of the literature on the subject, and finally make such insertions or revisions as my reading will give rise to. So long as I have not finished my own work I cannot read.'[31]

Even so Freud did not and could not have made a thorough study of the dream literature, or he would not have written: 'No one has the slightest suspicion that dreams are not nonsense but wish fulfillment.' Certainly there were many writers, Novalis, for example, and even

more significantly Gotthilf Heinrich von Schubert, who did not think
that dreams were 'nonsense'. Schubert wrote a most penetrating work
on dreams entitled *Die Symbolik des Traumes*, wherein he not only
anticipated Freud's theories but affirmed that, among other functions,
the dream served also that of wish fulfillment.[32]

It is not my intention to set up a gallery of pre-Freudians, nor to
challenge in any sense whatsoever Freud's claim to have been the sole
and original creator of psychoanalysis. I do intend, however, to underscore the fact that he was an optative autodidact, and that he 'discovered'
by dint of great labor the components of his metapsychology, which
components were already known, and defined, in many respects in
superior ways, in Romantic Medicine. That includes his dream interpretation, the Unconscious, repression, the Id, Ego, and Super-ego,
the concepts of Eros and Thanatos, and much else beside. I hasten to
add, however, that while all these add up to a great portion of Freud's
metapsychology, they do not add up to psychoanalysis as a psychologic
system or as a therapeutic procedure.

Psychoanalysis could not have been conceptualised in Romantic
Medicine, nor indeed at any time before the latter part of the nineteenth and the early part of the twentieth century. The reasons for
this are not difficult to fathom. They are akin to those reasons which
brought forth vitamin therapy in the twentieth century, and not before. Vitamin therapy, as is well known, provides the metabolic
mechanism, in the second instance, with that of which it was deprived
in the first instance. Until foods were subjected to refinements, that is
to devitaminising processes and to other corrupting influences, there
was no compelling necessity for a science of vitamins nor for vitamin
therapy. The metapsychology upon which Freud based his psychoanalysis was an integral component of Romantic Medicine, and there
was no necessity to extricate it into a separate discipline. That necessity
arose only when medicine was subjected to the dismemberment and
disorientation it experienced under the influence of the French rationalistic science and in the so-called school of von Helmholtz.

I fear this argument may be misunderstood, that it may be taken for
a value judgement rather than as it is intended as the exposition of an
historical eventuation. I have a high regard for the philosophical
framework of Romantic Medicine but I do not esteem the actualities,
i.e. the practice of Romantic Medicine, nearly as high, nor in any

respect of effectiveness even remotely proximate to the medicine of today. I am certain, however, that none of the leading personages of the Romantic period – Goethe, Schelling, Carus, Oken, Novalis, Grimm, or Schubert, to name but a few, would find himself otherwise than at home in the labyrinthine metapsychology of psychoanalysis. I do suspect they would find some of it naive, but still very familiar. And as for the neurotic and psychotic patient, I would feel quite secure entrusting his treatment, say, to Schubert or to Damrow.

But to revert to Freud: it appears quite clear to me that in his long and intimate association with Fliess he was indoctrinated in the ideational framework of a relatedness system – closely akin to that of Romantic Medicine, and that within this framework, which he singly and laboriously reconstructed, he worked out both the metapsychology and the operational patterns of psychoanalysis.

The break between Fliess and Freud, no matter how it may have been marked by overt events, took place when Freud, starting off from their commonly shared terrain of ideas and convictions, departed in his unique direction. Fliess understandably felt abandoned and denied, and he counted Freud an ingrate. Freud on his part was too feverishly preoccupied in the pursuit of his own concerns to allow himself the distractions of a friendship that had already given him its all. But that Fliess had indoctrinated and nurtured Freud in the philosophy of 'world and man relatedness', there can be no doubt. Fliess' frustration was in a measure that of the hen that had brooded and hatched a duckling.

Freud, started on the pursuit of his metapsychology, could not and would not be deflected. In December 1897 Freud wrote that he was keenly looking forward to meeting with Fliess 'and the fine things you will have to tell me about life and its dependence on the world process. I have always been curious about it, but hitherto I have never found any one who could give me an answer'. And to this he added, and not in jest, 'If there are now two people, one of whom can say what life is, and the other can say (nearly) what mind is, it is only right that they should see and talk to each other more often.'[33] But in March of 1900 Freud was quite of a different mind. He declined Fliess' proposal that they meet at Easter, and gave a motley of explanations for his declinations. 'Subtle resolution of contradictions', 'inner reasons, – an accumulation of imponderables, which weighed heavily upon him', and so on – all of it adding up to the fact that he had no more use for Fliess. He was henceforth on his own.

There would be little profit in tracing Freud's psychoanalytic architectonics – the sequence in which he constructed his theoretical edifice – Jones has done that laboriously. It *is* of interest, however, to take note that his first, major, and in the opinion of many, his most significant work, was composed when he was still friendly with Fliess. The work was his *Interpretation of Dreams*. How did Freud come to make this study, to compose this work, so substantive in Romantic Medicine? In *Zur Geschichte der Psychoanalytischen Bewegung*[34] Freud states that he came upon dream interpretation 'nachdem ich mich, einer dunklen Ahnung folgend, entschlossen hatte die Hypnose mit der freien Assoziation zu vertauschen' ('after I had resolved, following a vague inspiration, to substitute for hypnosis free association'). 'My thirst for knowledge', he adds, 'had not initially been directed towards the understanding of dreams. I do not know of any influences that directed my interest or gave me helpful expectation.'

One is prompted to wonder – is this but another instance of Freud's amnestic slips? He did praise old Fechner for his understanding of dreams and Fechner, it should be noted, was a distinguished Romantic.

Two items remain to be dealt with: the reaction of the world of science to Freud's theories, and the phenomenal fact that despite great opposition they have substantially 'prevailed', that is, they have received discrete, critical, but none-the-less effective acceptance in medicine and in psychiatry. As to the first, the fiction has been propagated that Freud met opposition chiefly because of his sex theories. Essentially this was not the case though it should be added that Freud's 'sex theories', on their own, and apart from all other evocative factors, did arouse the sceptical derision of the scientific world. And well they might. The 'sexuality' of current day psychoanalysis is quite different from that hypothesized by Freud in the 1890s and early 1900s. Much of that difference is glossed over in the psychoanalytical records of the reception given to Freud's early and initial formulations. But vastly more significant is the historic fact that Freud's theories were opposed and challenged on the score that they were not scientific, that they were wild to the point of being a 'bad joke' (P. Janet). Wilfred Trotter wrote:

However much one may be impressed by the greatness of the edifice which Freud has built up, and by the soundness of his architecture, one can scarcely fail, on coming into it from the bracing atmosphere of the biological sciences, to be oppressed by the odour of humanity with which it is pervaded. One finds everywhere a tendency to the acceptance of human standards and even sometimes of human pretensions, which cannot fail to produce a certain uneasiness as to the validity, if not of his doctrines, at any rate of the forms in which they are expounded.[35]

Oswald Bumke wrote: 'You may define science as you please. *Psychoanalysis is not natural science nor any kind of science*, nor is it a fairy tale. For unlike the latter, it does not spring from the heart, but rather from a coldly brooding and yet misguided intellect.'[36]

Freud's system was indeed not science, as science was then known, but rather 'reeked of humanity'. It was not science for it dealt with imponderables lacking the accustomed dimensions of the accredited data of science. It reeked of humanity with all of humanity's ephemerities. It treated of hopes, aims, ambitions, goals, frustrations – the subjectivistic corruptions that encumber the operations of the undisciplined mind – the dross of human mentation which more than a century before had been fused off and discarded as so much slag in the crucibles of science.

Freud himself was cognisant of his scientific apostasy. In his *Introductory Lectures*[37] he warns his auditors that in order to grasp the burden of his intentions they will need, indeed will be required, to shed their indoctrinated and habituated patterns of thinking, perceiving, and testing, and that the very nature of proof in psychoanalysis will be such as must of necessity run contrary to their ingrained expectations.

Freud and his psychoanalysis stood forth as an offence against the objectivity and purity of science, and they were resented deeply and bitterly. And yet, they both prevailed. How many, different, elements entered into the ultimate acceptance of psychoanalysis among the confraternity of learned disciplines, I cannot at this time undertake to catalogue or to describe. Two factors, however, stand forth above all others. Freud's personality, his Promethean drive and obdurate endurance, and, the fundamental pertinence of the reorientation of man to himself, to the experience of growth and development, and to the intricate adventures of living, implicit in Freud's metapsychology, and in much of the technique of psychoanalysis.

It is most questionable whether psychoanalysis as we know it, historically and practically, would have come into being had there not been a Freud to bring it into being. But even at the time of Freud there was more than a nascent suspicion that matter and energy, substance and motion, physics and chemistry, and all the rest in accepted science, would not suffice to explicate all the phenomena and experiences witnessed in life. Indeed science itself had come under scrutiny and its basic assumptions were being challenged by science proper. It is relevant to recall that Michelson's crucial experiment on the velocity of light was made in 1881, and repeated in 1887 and 1905. Einstein wrote his initial work on Relativity in 1905, and the Curies conducted their unique studies on the pitch blende in 1898.

There was prevalent a valence of receptivity for the insight Freud brought to the realm of biology in general, and to psychology in particular. It is understandable that Freud and his partisans underscore the opposition he encountered. Historically, however, the acceptance of his ideas is even more noteworthy, and the acceptance was of no mean proportion. Holt spoke for many of his contemporaries when he said of Freud's work: 'It is the first key which psychology has ever had which fitted' (*The Freudian Wish*). The 'key that fits' is a happy phrase. It is the key we name by many names – ecological, holistic, ethological. It is in essence the key to the understanding of the universe and to man's relation to it – the crude blank of which was proffered more than a century ago – in Romantic Medicine.

I cannot terminate this presentation without speculating, however briefly, on what might have been the state of psychiatry today – had Freud never lived and never labored. I am persuaded that while we would not have had psychoanalysis as a discipline and movement, with all that this implies of good and bad, psychiatric knowledge, psychiatric theory, and psychiatric practice would in all vital essentials not have been any different from what they are currently. I am impelled, but I am not happy, to thus commit myself. I am sure to be misunderstood, and likely to be abused. Oddly enough I could with impunity and general assent say as much about other great personages in the history of science, of say Darwin, or Copernicus. But Freud is quite another matter! He stands unique! That is quite correct and it is precisely the point I want to make. Freud *is* historically unique – *in his personality*. None but Freud could have been Freud. But others could, and most likely would have done the fundamental work, contributed by Freud. Freud has been compared to Darwin, to Newton, and to Copernicus. I concur in these comparisons. Yet to my mind there is but one man he truly resembles – not in any other respect – but in the signature of his personality – that man is Paracelsus. The motto of his life was: *Alterius not sit, qui suus esse potest.* Freud elected no motto, but the one he inscribed on the Frontispiece of his *Interpretation of Dreams* characterises the passionate ambition that characterises his life and his work:

FLECTERE SI NEQUEO SUPEROS, ACHERONTA MOVEBO. (Virg.)
('If I cannot influence the gods of heaven, I will stir up Acheron itself.')
I will avail myself of every possible resource to accomplish my purpose.

It is my profound conviction that long after all that is sound and valid in his system of psychoanalysis has been absorbed and incorporated in psychiatry, Freud will be prized and celebrated above all else for the heroic dimensions of his being, for the valiance of his character, and for his Promethean spirit.

SOURCE: *Bulletin of The History of Medicine,* **xxx** (1956).

NOTES

1. I premise neither calculated neglect nor wilful suppression of any essential data. It is rather that Freud's biographers in the first instance were not aware of the quality and nature of Freud's friendship with Fliess, and Jones, who has written with the benefit of the Fliess letters, and much else beside, is either ignorant of, or too little concerned with, the philosophical and historical implications of the ideas so intimately shared by Freud and Fliess during the fifteen years of their association, years which confessedly were formative for Freud.

2. Sigmund Freud, *Aus den Anfängen der Psychoanalyse. Briefe an Wilhelm Fliess, Abhandlungen und Notizen aus den Jahren 1887–1902* (London, 1950).

3. Jones vs Jones – 'Of more lasting assistance was that rendered by Dr Wilhelm Fliess, whom Abraham got to know a few years later and for whom he conceived a great regard; it was Fliess who was mainly responsible for his treatment during his last illness', from Ernest Jones's Introduction to *Selected Papers of Karl Abraham* (London, 1927) p. 12.

Again in Jones's *Life and Work of Sigmund Freud,* vol. 1 (New York, 1953): 'Of those who knew him (Fliess), with the exception of the level-headed Karl Abraham, who was not impressed, everyone speaks of his "fascinating" personality.'

4. Fritz Wittels, *Sigmund Freud* (E. P. Tal & Co. Verlag, 1924).

5. Siegfried Bernfeld, 'Freud's Scientific Beginning', *The American Imago,* vol. 6, no. 3 (Sept. 1949).

6. Ernest Jones, *The Life and Work of Sigmund Freud*, vol. I (New York, 1953) p. xii.

7. Ibid. p. xiii.

8. Ibid. p. 78.

9. Bernfeld, op. cit.

10. Jones, op. cit. p. 168.

11. Sigmund Freud, *Aus den Anfängen der Psychoanalyse. Briefe an Wilhelm Fliess* (London, 1950) p. 18: 'In einem zufällig erhaltenen Briefe Breuers an Fliess aus dem Sommer' 1895, mehrere Monate vor dem Erscheinen der "Studien über Hysterie" heisst es: "Freud ist im vollsten Schwung seines Intellekts. Ich sehe ihm schon nach wie die Henne dem Falken."'

The above quotation is corrupted in the English translation to read, 'Freud's intellect is soaring; I struggle along behind him like a hen behind a hawk.' Fancy a hen struggling along behind a hawk!

12. Sigmund Freud, 'An Autobiographical Study', translated by James Strachey in *The Problems of Lay-analysis* (New York, 1952).

13. Only one brief note has survived.

14. And as Fliess observed with some pathos: 'Mit Freud stand ich jahrelang in freundschaftlichem Verkehr. Ihm habe ich alle meine wissenschaftlichen Gedanken und Keime rückhaltlos anvertraut.' *Der Ablauf des Lebens* (Leipzig und Wien, 1906) p. 583.

15. For a more ample treatment of Romantic Medicine, see Iago Galdston, 'The Romantic Period in Medicine', *Bulletin of The New York Academy of Medicine*, vol. 32, no. 5 (May 1956).

16. Ernst Cassirer, *The Philosophy of the Enlightenment*, translated by Fritz C. A. Koelln and James P. Pettegrove (Boston, 1955) p. 65.

17. Ibid. p. 88.

18. Ibid. p. 83.

19. To study nature is to project one's self into, 'to sympathize with nature, to trace the likeness between the inner life and the magnets, the crystals, the solar systems, the living creatures of the physical world.' Josiah Royce, *The Spirit of Modern Philosophy* (New York, 1931) p. 175.

20. 1817–35: *Isis; oder, Enzyklopaedische Zeitung* (Jena und Leipzig). Edited by L. Oken. Originally a political periodical until 1824, it changed title to *Enzyklopädische Zeitschrift vorzüglich für Naturgeschichte*, etc.

21. Sigmund Freud, *Aus den Anfängen der Psychoanalyse. Briefe an Wilhelm Fliess, Abhandlungen und Notizen aus den Jahren 1887–1902* (London, 1950) p. 40.

22. Wilhelm Fliess, *Der Ablauf des Lebens. Grundlegung zur exakten Biologie* (Leipzig und Wien, 1906).

23. Life expectancy at given ages is currently estimated, and accepted.

24. Werner Leibbrand, *Romantische Medizin* (Hamburg und Leipzig, 1937) p. 65.

25. Gerhard Stengel, *Die Deutschen Romantiker*, vol. I, 'Die Zahl' (Salzburg, 1954) p. 623.

26. Ernst Hirschfeld, 'Romantische Medizin,' in *Kyklos*, vol. 3 (Leipzig, 1930) p. 14.

27. Stengel, op. cit., p. 640.

28. Sigmund Freud, *The Origins of Psycho-analysis, Letters to Wilhelm Fliess*, translation by Mosbacher and Strachey (New York, 1954) p. 126, Letter 29.

29. Ibid. p. 157, Letter 41.

30. Ibid. p. 187, Letter 56.

31. Ibid. p. 249, Letter 86.

32. Gotthilf Heinrich von Schubert, *Die Symbolik des Traumes* (F. A. Brockhaus, 1862) p. 19.

33. Sigmund Freud, *The Origins of Psycho-analysis, Letters to Wilhelm Fliess*, translation by Mosbacher and Strachey, p. 238, Letter 79.

34. Sigmund Freud, *Zur Geschichte der Psychoanalytischen Bewegung* (Leipzig, Wien, Zürich, 1924) p. 16.

35. Wilfred Batten Lewis Trotter, *Instincts of the Herd in Peace and War*, (New York, 1919) pp. 77–8.

36. Bernard Sachs, M.D., 'Bumke's Critique of Psychoanalysis, *Mental Hygiene*, vol. XVI, no. 3 (July 1932) pp. 409–27.

37. Sigmund Freud, *Introductory Lectures on Psycho-analysis*, English translation by Joan Rivière (London, 1922).

IDA MACALPINE

Tribute to Freud (1956)

THE one hundredth anniversary of Freud's birth finds his ideas generally embodied in our daily life: we speak of wishful thinking and of having something in the back of our minds. In the field of psychiatry, however, the passage of time has not yet afforded that distance which is necessary for objective assessment and a verdict on which all psychiatrists may agree. In fact, opinion is sharply divided about the value of psychoanalysis, and a wide gap separates partisan psychoanalysts and the main body of clinical psychiatrists. There are still a great many workers in this field who disparage depth or dynamic psychology and who believe that behaviouristic data and the manifestations of the conscious mind alone provide legitimate and reliable sources of information. Contrasted with them are the psychoanalytic schools for whom psychoanalysis contains the solution of all problems – a kind of be-all and end-all of psychiatry.

I shall not speak of Freud the man, nor of his achievements as a neurologist; Ernest Jones's *Sigmund Freud: Life and Work* gives all the available information. Nor will I have time to consider psychoanalysis from the philosophical point of view, nor its application to other fields such as anthropology, art, folklore, religion, and so on. I propose to limit myself to an historical examination of the development of psychoanalysis, touching here and there on points of contact or discord between it and clinical psychiatry. In this way one may hope to arrive at an assessment of Freud's contribution to the science of the mind, that is to psychiatry, which would satisfy a speaker at the Osler Club standing in my place in another hundred years' time.

I enter the arena of conflict over psychoanalysis neither to praise nor to bury Freud, but in the endeavour to appraise his work. This is perhaps the most reverential way of paying tribute to one who was a courageous seeker of the truth, however unpalatable. He had little

regard for hero-worship, and often derided man's innate urge to bow
to authority and tradition rather than think and observe for himself.
He admired Charcot's words, 'Look at things again and again and
facts will eventually emerge and speak to you.'

I must, at the outset, clarify a confusion which besets much of the
argument about the value of psychoanalysis. The term, although
synonymous with Freud's work, is used with three entirely different
meanings. First, it is used to describe a psychology which acknow-
ledges the existence of a dynamic unconscious; second, it is used for
the great theoretical superstructure – the libido theory – which Freud
built up on his early clinical observations in the attempt to establish
a complete and systematic normal and abnormal psychology; third, it is
applied to the classical technique of psychoanalysis as a form of psychological treatment. I propose to deal with these in turn. Of course, in
asserting that there are three different issues at stake, I at once reveal
my provenance, because a professional psychoanalyst would hardly
agree that psychoanalysis is divisible. Indeed it is remarkable and one
of the paradoxes in the history of 'movements' that psychoanalysis,
which started as a rebellion against formalised psychiatric tradition,
has itself in its comparatively short life developed an almost unassailable orthodoxy and intolerance. This makes contact between psychiatrist and psychoanalyst almost impossible, to the disadvantage of
both.

I THE UNCONSCIOUS

Although all branches of science profit by being studied historically,
the only way to understand the present position of psychoanalysis is
by study of its historical background and development. It is often
assumed that Freud discovered the unconscious mind. This is not so,
and was often denied by Freud himself. The idea of an unconscious
beyond the conscious mind is found scattered throughout the whole of
the nineteenth century. To mention only a few: Herbart, seventy years
before Freud, spoke of unconscious processes, even of a dynamic
unconscious dominated by constant conflict: he also used the term
'repressed' for an idea which is driven out of, or is unable to reach,
consciousness because of an opposing idea. In the 1830s there was
animated controversy between two eminent British physicians,
Professor Laycock and Dr Carpenter, over priority of the term

'unconscious cerebration'. In 1873 Sir James Paget discussed cases of 'nervous mimicry' as arising from 'unconscious mental association'. Lipps, whose writings were well known to Freud, wrote in 1883, 'We maintain not merely the existence of unconscious processes beside the conscious ones; we postulate further that unconscious processes are the basis of conscious ones and accompany them.' The knowledge that dreams and insanity are of the same stuff dates from the time of the Greek philosophers. In Hughlings Jackson's words, 'Find out about dreams and you will find out about insanity.' This of course implies acceptance of dynamic unconscious processes.

Such views were not received as startling novelties, nor did they arouse the criticisms later levelled against Freud when he put the unconscious on the map. But the recognition of a vague unconscious mind did not help the understanding of mental processes and therefore could play no part in psychiatry.

This was the situation in 1885 when Freud emerged ready to start practice as a fully trained neurologist. A patient presented who could not walk or stand: was he suffering from neurological disease or was his mind disordered? This fundamental and perennial problem, to which Freud had already contributed an important paper, was less clear-cut and more difficult at a time when neurology lacked many essential techniques of investigation, even the plantar reflex. And what was to be done with the host of patients whose symptoms obviously did originate in the mind? What was so-called hysteria and how did it arise? In order to find out Freud went to Paris to attend Charcot's famous lectures at the Salpêtrière, where 'la grande hystérie' was demonstrated in a big way and symptoms produced by hypnosis. This seemed to show that so-called hysteria was an affection of the mind and not a disease of the nerves. Freud was enthusiastic about the seriousness with which Charcot studied this subject. On his return to Vienna he read a paper to the Medical Society which was coldly received. Interest in psychology was not particularly respectable, and Freud was soon to make it less so. But he was now on the road he was never to leave again.

From an older colleague, Breuer, he heard of the now historic case of Miss Anna O., who under daily hypnosis recalled traumatic events of her past with great emotion: with each recollection some of her symptoms disappeared. The patient herself called this procedure the 'talking cure'. She was said to have 'abreacted' and the treatment became known as the cathartic method. Three lessons were learnt: that unconscious material could be recalled, that this was accompanied by the release of affect, and that this in turn had a therapeutic effect. From these early findings psychoanalysis gradually developed.

Free Association

Freud soon found hyponosis unsatisfactory, not only because he disliked its monotony, but because many patients could not be hypnotised. He continued having the patient lie on the couch, but desisted from making hypnotic suggestions. Instead he urged the patient to relate freely what was passing through his mind without suppressing or censoring anything. So was born 'free association', the hallmark of the new technique of psychoanalysis, later known as the 'fundamental rule'. In applying it Freud observed that what had always appeared as an haphazard, unconnected and almost incoherent medley of ideas, turned out to be linked together into a chain of thoughts, the link being an unconscious association determined by a traceable 'complex'. This was Freud's most momentous discovery: the unconscious link in our associations. The physician now became the analyst, and his task to detect and make known to the patient the unconscious meaning of his conscious thoughts. This was called interpretation. Tracing out associations led back to the traumatic experience, which Freud then – still following Charcot – considered responsible for the symptom. Thus with one bold stroke he introduced into the clinically sterile academic association psychology of his time a living principle. Before Freud, association of ideas had been studied experimentally by philosophers, physicians, and psychologists, who formulated laws governing them in terms of continuity, contiguity, similarity, and so on. Freud's discovery of an unconscious link cut across these fetters and established a dynamic psychology no longer confined to superficial cognitive data and isolated phenomena. By patient study of the free flow of associations he had discovered the bridge across which the interplay of conscious and unconscious mental operations could be observed. In this way he was able to unravel the processes of the dynamic unconscious, and so made possible direct, that is scientific, observation of the workings of the mind.

Dreams

From here it was but one step to what Freud himself always regarded
as his greatest discovery: he had noticed that patients related dreams,
and then that these became meaningful when the ideas preceding and
following were noted. The most absurd dream was seen to fit into the
context of the patient's associations and through them could be understood. Interest in dreams is, of course, as old as mankind, but never
before had their study revealed the workings of the mind. When
Freud made the dream language intelligible by translating its absurd
manifest content into its latent meaning, interpretation of dreams
became 'the royal road' to the unconscious. Indeed Freud considered
his book, *Interpretation of Dreams*, in 1900 his magnum opus.

Freud soon found that unconscious ideas reveal themselves in other
ways: by slips of the tongue and by parapraxes. That we feel embarras-
sed on such occasions is due to the realisation that they reveal our
innermost thoughts. There is the story of the unwilling chairman who
opened a meeting after a few introductory remarks with the words:
'I now have great pleasure in declaring this meeting closed.'

 psychic determinism

Transference

To these ways and means by which unconscious content can be
followed, and which were the fruits of the methods of free association,
Freud early on added one more fundamental discovery: transference
phenomena. This was to become the second cornerstone of psychoanalysis. One day – to Freud's consternation – a patient fell round his
neck. He concluded that patients react to the analyst as if he were a
figure of their past; without seeming provocation they would in turn
love, hate, admire, and deride him. These unconscious feelings were
often of a disturbing nature and hence Freud considered them pathogenic. They could not be recalled by will or conscious effort, but
returned as transference manifestations in the analytic session. In this
way they became conscious, open to inspection, and could be analysed
and ventilated.

Through the medium of free association, and dream and transference
analysis, Freud was able to elucidate mechanisms of the unconscious
such as projection, denial, sublimation, identification, and others.

Summarising: of the greatest importance during what may be

called Freud's first period was the discovery and development of a new technique for investigating the operations of the mind. It was, in fact, the only methodological advance ever made in psychology, either before or after Freud. By being made amenable to observation, mental symptoms were no longer obscure and bizarre but could be studied and so understood.

Self-analysis

The instrument of the new technique was the therapist's own mind. When Freud gave up the hypnotist's activities and substituted the observing, non-interfering analyst, he realised – good psychologist that he was – that the analyst's personal and unconscious difficulties are likely to color his observations, and that he might turn a deaf ear to what is repellent to him. He therefore turned his mind on to his own mind and heroically embarked on a self-analysis. Over several years he wrote down his dreams and fearlessly associated to them. From then on, understanding of his own mind became a prerequisite for the analyst. From the relatively modest demand developed the obligatory training analysis of the analyst, which in the course of time has assumed much wider significance. Indeed, it is now a major dividing line between psychoanalyst and psychiatrist. While Freud maintained to the last that a vivid dreamer could, with perseverance, conduct his own analysis, most psychoanalytic societies now demand a training analysis of not less than four years. Its aims have become so ambitious as to be unrealistically idealistic: a training analysis is by no means foolproof, in fact often the reverse. Prolonged personal contact between analyst and analysand in the rarefied analytic atmosphere tends to create dependent indoctrinated disciples rather than free and independent pupils and so defeats its own purpose. More serious is the belief that a personal analysis can in any way replace all-round training in clinical psychiatry as a branch of medicine. While the danger of this shift of value has been recognised in America, where psychiatric training is obligatory for the professional analyst, in England it is not even demanded that the analyst be medically qualified. Naturally, this discredits any claim of psychoanalysis to be a science and further widens the gulf between it and clinical psychiatry. Nevertheless, the principle of some personal training in the understanding of the workings of his own mind is essential for every worker in this field. This is not just a

Freudian whim. As early as 1798 Alexander Crichton in his book *An Inquiry into the Nature and Origin of Mental Derangement* wrote: 'It is evidently required that he who undertakes this branch of science ... should be acquainted with the human mind ... and should be capable of abstracting his own mind from himself, and placing it before him, as it were.' One of the urgent tasks facing psychiatry today is to devise personal training facilities without the ambitious and exorbitant demands in time, money, and energy of formal training analysis, and without implicit allegiance to psychoanalytic schools.

II   THE LIBIDO THEORY

I have taken considerable time in tracing the milestones of Freud's early period, because by 1900 he had made most of the clinical observations which represent the imperishable content and essence of his work. He had laid the foundation for a psychology of the mind: later findings are foreshadowed, and much of later theory anticipated. I come now to the libido theory which Freud built up and elaborated to explain his early clinical findings and by which he maintained psychoanalysis stands or falls.

To appreciate the significance of this intricate system, and Freud's lifelong efforts to straighten it out, we must pause to glance at Freud, the man. His personality combined two almost diametrically opposed qualities. On the one hand he was a fearless, original, sensitive observer with a flair for seeing things never seen before. As such he is timeless. But he was also an inveterate and ambitious systematiser, and here he is dated. Freud's so-called Fliess period affords astounding examples of this side of his character. In the further development of psychoanalysis the emphasis was placed on theory, to the neglect of fresh clinical observations, perhaps because Freud saw his discoveries and his theory as one inseparable body of knowledge.

Strenuous efforts are still being made to reconcile the facts with the theory, and to fit observation into hypothesis. Few important clinical observations have been made other than those made by Freud himself. Hypothetical assumptions are taken for clinical facts and concepts treated as objective data. This is what makes much psychoanalytic literature sound like scholastic disputations which the outsider finds almost unreadable. Significantly, with the formation of psychoanalytic schools, Freud is no longer quoted as having made an observation but as having made a pronouncement.

The libido theory was intended to explain systematically the first fruits of the observations made by the new psychoanalytic method. Freud had been struck by the regularity with which sexual traumata were related by patients, and he soon came to consider all symptoms as the return of the repressed in disguised form. The repressed itself, the unconscious, was a sexual wish which was denied gratification by an opposing, censoring force, later called the superego. The unconscious instinctual drive became the Id; to which later again was added that elusive structure, the ego. Superego and Id were the contending forces of the classical Freudian conflict, which in turn was considered the basis of symptom formation. Freud now postulated that all symptoms were wish fulfilments of sexual drives and extended this hypothesis from the milder disturbances, the psychoneuroses with which psychoanalysis mainly deals, to the severer, the psychoses.

Mental Apparatus

Freud's theories mark him as the child of his time. To sketch their background, if only in roughest outline, is not only of academic interest; many of the neurophysiological and neuroanatomical views and concepts of the second half of the nineteenth century live on and determine psychoanalytic thought today. Although Freud's great merit is that he went further than anybody before him in building up a psychology of the mind, the mind itself was conceived as a 'mental apparatus', a reflex arc dealing with stimuli from within and without. Influenced by Helmholtz, Fechner, Bruecke, and Meynert, Freud thought in terms of quantitative nervous energy; he based his deductions on Fechner's law of constancy according to which the functions of the mental apparatus are governed by the principle of keeping excitation at a constant level. Any increase in excitation was pictured as seeking immediate discharge; if its path was blocked, it flowed back into the central apparatus. Hence many psychoanalytic terms, such as discharge, blocked affect, damming-up of libido, which are survivals of the neurophysiology of that time. This is well shown by a recent example in a respectable psychoanalytic publication: 'The energy which was withdrawn from the dangerous urge evaporates in forming the hallucination . . . which therefore is a discharge phenomenon.'

Such statements make sense only as relics of an outmoded neuro-physiology, but are psychologically meaningless. Of course the term psychoneurosis itself was used to emphasise that mind and nerves are subject to the same laws and their energies interchangeable.

Instincts

On this model of the mental apparatus it was easy to account for stimuli from without, but not from within. Freud accepted the current theory of instincts and for his own purposes reduced them to two: the self-preservative or ego instinct and the species-preservative or sexual instinct. In common parlance, hunger and love make the world go round. As Freud had been impressed by the frequency with which patients recounted sexual wishes and fantasies, the sexual drive and its vicissitudes became the center of psychoanalytic theory – hence libido theory. Sexual libido became the fuel with which the human machine is kept going, and all symptoms were visualised as wish fulfilments of sexual drives. In this way the oedipus complex became the 'nuclear complex' of all neuroses. Symptom formation was generalised into the series: sexual impulse – opposing forbidding forces – conflict – repression – faulty repression – discharge of the energy attached to the repressed wish in disguised form, which was the symptom. When the energy attached to the repressed wish finds discharge into motor paths – as in so-called hysterical paralysis – nervous energy was thought to be converted into physical energy; hence Freud termed it 'conversion hysteria'. This is the libido theory, the basis and essence of which Freud never relinquished.

But not all the clinical facts fitted. Freud's next step was to enlarge the meaning of 'sexual'. In his *Three Essays on the Theory of Sexuality* (1905) he spoke of partial or component instincts of infantile sexuality and of 'erotogenic zones', obviously inspired by Charcot's romantic 'hysterogenic zones'. In 1911 he attempted to apply his theory for the first time to the psychoses, when he analysed the classic Schreber Memoirs. He was forced to amend the libido theory and announced to a 'bewildered group of analysts' – I quote Jones – in his book *On Narcissism* (1914) that the ego itself is endowed with sexuality, be-cause man can also take himself as love-object narcissistically. This, he surmised somewhat naïvely, was what psychotics must do when their libido is withdrawn from the outside world. This was the second libido theory. A more fundamental change had to be made in the 1920s, beginning with 'Beyond the Pleasure Principle'. Having committed himself once and for all to the doctrine of wish fulfilment as the cause of symptoms and adhering to the constancy principle, Freud now postulated a different set of instincts: one of aggression, the death instinct or thanatos, and an instinct of love, eros. This was the third version of the libido theory. Obviously these changes meant, and still mean much recasting of earlier views and formulations; this may account for the previously remarked preponderance of theoretical over clinical writings in psychoanalytic literature.

Regression

Thus Freud's libido theory is seen to have been erected on nineteenth century neuroanatomical and neurophysiological concepts. It further reflects the profound influence exerted on Freud by Darwin's theory of evolution. From it he derived the concept of regression in the face of conflict to earlier, more primitive, levels. Regression meant recapitulation in reverse order of earlier stages of mental or sexual development. In this Freud followed closely Hughlings Jackson's similar concept in neurological disease of dissolution as reversal of evolution. Whereas in the natural sciences the recapitulation theory is being modified, if not abandoned, it has remained axiomatic in psychoanalysis that patients regress to, or are fixated at, primitive levels of development and to seek the origin of adult symptoms in ever earlier infancy. Freud expressed this in his dictum 'no neurosis without an infantile neurosis', and extended it to explain all psychiatric symptoms, including those of the most severely disturbed, although these could not be investigated – for obvious reasons – by the couch-free association technique. Although the concept of psychic regression is treated as established fact, indeed as a psychoanalytic *sine qua non* of all morbid symptoms, although it made an indelible impression on psychoanalytic treatment by prolonging it indefinitely, and although it has entered psychiatric jargon, it is well to remember that we are not dealing with an established law, but with an attempted explanation based on dated theory.

Here we must leave the libido theory. Whatever the final verdict on it may be, there are immediate practical implications. Of the many I shall mention only two. The concept of regression led to labels for patients such as immature, passive, and dependent, which are not clinical diagnoses and have no clinical value as they reveal nothing of the dynamics of the patient's mind; by all too readily implying moral judgement, they are often worse than useless. Despite, or because of, their vagueness and arbitrariness, these labels have found their way into common use in psychiatry, especially into that branch called psychosomatic medicine where they are used to describe fictitious personality types. The second consequence of a theory which places the roots of all mental illness in earliest childhood – the British school of psychoanalysis believes that the oedipus complex operates in the first year of life – is to deny the possibility and hence to discourage attempts at short and serious psychotherapy.

III   THE CLASSICAL TECHNIQUE OF PSYCHOANALYSIS

This brings me to my third topic: psychoanalysis as a form of treatment. The principle features are: the patient reclines on the couch; the analyst sits behind him out of sight and his activity is confined to interpretation; sessions last fifty minutes and take place regularly six times a week. These rules were not established by trial and error, nor did they result from experiments to discover the best technique. Their historical development shows them to be survivals of the past: one may therefore appropriately speak of the 'analytic ritual'. For example, from the beginning Freud insisted on six sessions per week, probably because after his first glimpses of the unconscious he feared he might lose contact with it unless he saw the patient daily. I may remark in passing that when psychoanalysis came to England and the demands of the week-end automatically reduced the number of weekly sessions to five, no untoward effects were reported. The technique is a tradition, its individual features are ill-understood, and have never been scientifically investigated. This explains the noteworthy fact that no history of the technique has yet been written.

Findings derived from observations made during analysis are based on the traditional assumption that the technique is a passive, registering instrument and the analyst merely a mirror: the patient's associations are accordingly considered spontaneous and to reveal his unconscious in pure culture. But the technique is not the passive instrument it is thought and jealously taught to be. Even if the analyst could be entirely passive, this passivity itself together with the analytic ritual are bound to exert a profound influence on the patient; and the interpretations given him must color his trend of thought. The more the analyst interprets in terms of infancy, the more infantile material the patient will produce. The same may be said about sex. The absolute authority the analyst demands naturally facilitates a father transference, so that it cannot even be maintained that the oedipus complex always appears unaided.

This indeed is the crux of the matter: the classical technique yielded the theory, and the theory in turn moulded and hardened the technique. Theory and technique reinforce each other, because historically they are inseparable, almost a vicious circle. But as the technique is not a passive instrument, observations obtained by it will have to be revised to allow for the influence it exerts on the patient. Much of what passes now for clinical evidence from the couch may turn out to be artefact.

The more the theory was enlarged, the more analyses were prolonged, paradoxically, because with growing experience one could have hoped treatment might be shortened. Why did the early three months' analyses yield results? In the 1930s the majority lasted under eighteen months, and many only six months. Perhaps because analyses now go on for so many years, a myth has arisen in the lay mind, which is spreading to the medical profession, that psychoanalysis is the most complete and radical form of psychotherapy, a kind of luxury reserved for the few. Even if this were so – and there is no evidence that it is – the possible benefit derived by the few would fall far short of the incalculable harm done to the many for whom the development of shorter techniques based on sound understanding of the unconscious is the only hope of psychiatric help.

Results of Treatment

The demand has therefore been voiced that analysts publish their results, so that the value of psychoanalysis as a form of treatment may be assessed. But in this field the evaluation of treatment results is even more unsatisfactory and unreliable than in other medical disciplines, because a large proportion of psychiatric patients get better with or without treatment. Much more information could be gained from close scrutiny of failures and aggravations, which indeed may contain the clue to many unsolved problems. Here one cannot spare the psychoanalytic schools the serious stricture that negative results have been passed over in silence; not even follow-up studies worthy of the name have been published. In similar circumstances Sir William Gull proposed that 'the greatest advance that could be made in practical science was to a full and intimate knowledge of our ignorance'.

There is not time to consider the effect of psychoanalysis on psychiatric classification. I would only like to make one point: that the classical technique is not applicable to psychotic patients has unfortunately led to the assumption that severely disturbed patients are beyond the pale of psychotherapy. Psychoanalysis has in this way tended to reinforce an altogether artificial division of mental illness into two fundamentally different kinds: the psychoneuroses and the psychoses. Much historical and clinical evidence could be brought forward to show that such a division is groundless, ignores the many transitional forms, and is a major stumbling block in the understanding of the psychopathology and hence psychotherapy of the psychoses.

CONCLUSION

In conclusion, to appreciate Freud's place in history means comparing him with the giants of science whom the judgement of time has given an assured place. Freud has been compared with Newton and Kepler, but I find it more congenial to remain within the natural sciences: to compare Freud with Harvey is perhaps most apt. Harvey, when he discovered the circulation of the blood, put an end to sterile speculation and static concepts which treated the body as if it were an assembly of loosely connected organs. In their place he gave us the notion of one functioning and organised organism, the mechanisms of which could be demonstrated and investigated. What Harvey did for the body, Freud did for the mind. Like Harvey, Freud cut the Gordian knot of barren scholastic tradition, and made his own observations. Harvey showed that the heart and blood were a vital economy, Freud observed the operations of the unconscious mind and demonstrated that they could be understood as a dynamic system of which conscious awareness and overt behaviour are only facets. The unconscious operations of the mind, which Freud was the first to demonstrate, were as little open to direct inspection as the circulation of the blood. Like Harvey's discovery, Freud's discovery was not created in a vacuum: both crystallised, by observation and experiment, ideas which were in the air; both had important precursors. As *De motu cordis* marked the beginning of a new era in science which made all subsequent knowledge of physiology and pathology possible, so Freud's work opened the way for the understanding of the mind, for a psycho-physiology and psycho-pathology. Neither was right in all his conclusions. How could they be? As Harvey lost nothing in stature by posterity finding that anastomoses between veins and arteries do exist although he had denied it, so will Freud's pioneer achievement not be belittled by parting from him in the details of the elaborate theoretical system he attempted to build up. Unfortunately, at the present time the official followers of Freud cling rigidly to his theoretical framework to the detriment of the great future advances made possible by his discoveries. Confusion of this superstructure with Freud's fundamental discovery explains the fact that one may still read disquisitions setting out to disprove Freud.

Harvey also had his adversaries. The learned Hoffmann in 1636 protested that Harvey

> Impeached and condemned Nature of folly and error, and that he had imputed to her the character of a most clumsy and inefficient artificer in suffering the blood to become recrudesent and making it return again and again to the heart . . . thus spoiling the perfectly made blood merely to find her something to do.

On a par with Hoffmann's spirited condemnation of the circulation of the blood are those psychiatrists and psychologists who brush aside the dynamic unconscious as a fanciful, useless artefact. Today it is as impossible to think of psychiatry without the dynamic unconscious as it is to think of medicine without the circulation of the blood. This is Freud's historic contribution.

SOURCE: A paper read at the Osler club, London on 22 March 1956; reprinted in *The Journal of the History of Medicine*, II (July 1956).

JEROME S. BRUNER

Freud and the Image of Man (1956)

By the dawn of the sixth century before Christ, the Greek physicist-philosophers had formulated a bold conception of the physical world as a unitary material phenomenon. The Ionics had set forth a conception of matter as fundamental substance, transformation of which accounted for the myriad forms and substances of the physical world. Anaximander was subtle enough to recognise that matter must be viewed as a generalised substance, free of any particular sensuous properties. Air, iron, water or bone were only elaborated forms, derived from a more general stuff. Since that time, the phenomena of the physical world have been conceived as continuous and monistic, as governed by the common laws of matter. The view was a bold one, bold in the sense of running counter to the immediate testimony of the senses. It has served as an axiomatic basis of physics for more than two millennia. The bold view eventually became the obvious view, and it gave shape to our common understanding of the physical world. Even the alchemists rested their case upon this doctrine of material continuity and, indeed, had they known about neutron bombardment, they might even have hit upon the proper philosopher's stone.

The good fortune of the physicist – and these matters are always relative, for the material monism of physics may have impeded nineteenth-century thinking and delayed insights into the nature of complementarity in modern physical theory – this early good fortune or happy insight has no counterpart in the sciences of man. Lawful continuity between man and the animal kingdom, between dreams and unreason on one side and waking rationality on the other, between madness and sanity, between consciousness and unconsciousness, between the mind of the child and the adult mind, between primitive and civilized man – each of these has been a cherished discontinuity preserved in doctrinal canons. There were voices in each generation, to be sure, urging the exploration of continuities. Anaximander had a passing good approximation to a theory of evolution based on natural selection; Cornelius Agrippa offered a plausible theory of the continuity of mental health and disease in terms of bottled-up sexuality. But Anaximander did not prevail against Greek conceptions of man's creation nor Cornelius Agrippa against the demonopathy of the *Malleus Maleficarum*. Neither in establishing the continuity between the varied states of man nor in pursuing the continuity between man and animal was there conspicuous success until the nineteenth century.

I need not insist upon the social, ethical, and political significance of an age's image of man, for it is patent that the view one takes of man affects profoundly one's standard of dignity and the humanly possible. And it is in the light of such a standard that we establish our laws, set our aspirations for learning, and judge the fitness of men's acts. Those who govern, then, must perforce be jealous guardians of man's ideas about man, for the structure of government rests upon an uneasy consensus about human nature and human wants. Since the idea of man is of the order of *res publica*, it is an idea not subject to change without public debate. Nor is it simply a matter of public concern. For man as individual has a deep and emotional investment in his image of himself. If we have learned anything in the last half-century of psychology, it is that man has powerful and exquisite capacities for defending himself against violations of his cherished self-image. This is not to say that Western man has not persistently asked: 'What is man that thou art mindful of him?' It is only that the question, when pressed, brings us to the edge of anxiety where inquiry is no longer free.

Two figures stand out massively as the architects of our present-day conception of man: Darwin and Freud. Freud's was the more daring, the more revolutionary, and in a deep sense, the more poetic insight. But Freud is inconceivable without Darwin. It is both timely and perhaps historically just to centre our inquiry on Freud's contribution to the modern image of man. Darwin I shall treat as a necessary condition for Freud and for his success, recognising, of course, that this is a form of psychological license. Not only is it the centenary of Freud's birth; it is also a year in which the current of popular thought expressed in commemoration of the date quickens one's awareness of Freud's impact on our times.

Rear-guard fundamentalism did not require a Darwin to slay it in an age of technology. He helped, but this contribution was trivial in comparison with another. What Darwin had done was to propose a set of principles unified around the conception that all organic species had their origins and took their form from a common set of circumstances – the requirements of biological survival. All living creatures were on a common footing. When the post-Darwin era of exaggeration had passed and religious literalism had abated into a new nominalism, what remained was a broad, orderly, and unitary conception of organic nature, a vast continuity from the mono-cellular protozoans to man. Biology had at last found its unifying principle in the doctrine of evolution. Man was not unique but the inheritor of an organic legacy.

As the summit of an evolutionary process, man could still view himself with smug satisfaction, indeed proclaim that God or Nature had shown a persistent wisdom in its effort to produce a final, perfect product. It remained for Freud to present the image of man as the unfinished product of nature: struggling against unreason, impelled by driving inner vicissitudes and urges that had to be contained if man were to live in society, host alike to seeds of madness and majesty, never fully free from an infancy anything but innocent. What Freud was proposing was that man at his best and man at his worst is subject to a common set of explanations: that good and evil grow from a common process.

Freud was strangely yet appropriately fitted for his role as architect of a new conception of man. We must pause to examine his qualifica-tions, for the image of man that he created was in no small measure founded on his painfully achieved image of himself and of his times. We are concerned not so much with his psychodynamics, as with the intellectual traditions he embodies. A child of his century's materialism, he was wedded to the determinism and the classical physicalism of nineteenth-century physiology so boldly represented by Helmholtz. Indeed, the young Freud's devotion to the exploration of anatomical structures was a measure of the strength of this inheritance. But at the same time, as both Lionel Trilling and W. H. Auden have recog-nized with much sensitivity, there was a deep current of romanticism in Freud – a sense of the role of impulse, of the drama of life, of the power of symbolism, of ways of knowing that were more poetic than rational in spirit, of the poet's cultural alienation. It was perhaps this romantic's sense of drama that led to his gullibility about parental seduction and to his generous susceptibility to the fallacy of the dramatic instance.

Freud also embodies two traditions almost as antithetical as romanticism and nineteenth-century scientism. He was profoundly a Jew, not in a doctrinal sense but in his conception of morality, in his love of the skeptical play of reason, in his distrust of illusion, in the form of his prophetic talent, even in his conception of mature eroticism. His prophetic talent was antithetic to a Utopianism either of innocence or of social control. Nor did it lead to a counsel of renunciation. Free oneself of illusion, of neurotic infantilism, and 'the soft voice of intellect' would prevail. Wisdom for Freud was neither doctrine nor formula, but the achievement of maturity. The patient who is cured is the one who is now free enough of neurosis to decide intelligently about his own destiny. As for his conception of mature love, it has always seemed to me that its blend of tenderness and sensuality combined the uxorious imagery of the Chassidic tradition and the sensual quality of the Song of Songs. And might it not have been Freud rather than a commentator of the Haftorahs who said, 'In children it was taught, God gives humanity a chance to make good its mistakes.' For the modern trend of permissiveness toward children is surely a feature of the Freudian legacy.

But for all the Hebraic quality, Freud is also in the classical tradition – combining the Stoics and the great Greek dramatists. For Freud as for the Stoics, there is no possibility of man disobeying the laws of nature. And yet, it is in this lawfulness that for him the human drama inheres. His love for Greek drama and his use of it in his formulation are patent. The sense of the human tragedy, the inevitable working out of the human plight – these are the hallmarks of Freud's case histories. When Freud, the tragic dramatist, becomes a therapist, it is not to intervene as a directive authority. The therapist enters the drama of the patient's life, makes possible a play within a play, the transference, and when the patient has 'worked through' and understood the drama, he has achieved the wisdom necessary for freedom. Again, like the Stoics, it is in the recognition of one's own nature and in the acceptance of the laws that govern it that the good life is to be found.

Freud's contribution lies in the continuities of which he made us aware. The first of these is the continuity of organic lawfulness. Accident in human affairs was no more to be brooked as 'explanation' than accident in nature. The basis for accepting such an 'obvious' proposition had, of course, been well prepared by a burgeoning nineteenth-century scientific naturalism. It remained for Freud to extend naturalistic explanation to the heart of human affairs. The *Psychopathology of Everyday Life* is not one of Freud's deeper works, but 'the Freudian slip' has contributed more to the common acceptance of lawfulness in human behavior than perhaps any of the more rigorous and academic formulations from Wundt to the present day. The forgotten lunch engagement, the slip of the tongue, the barked shin could no longer be dismissed as accident. Why Freud should have succeeded where the novelists, philosophers, and academic psychologists had failed we will consider in a moment.

Freud's extension of Darwinian doctrine beyond Haeckel's theorem that ontogeny recapitulates phylogeny is another contribution to continuity. It is the conception that in the human mind, the primitive, infantile, and archaic exist side-by-side with the civilised and evolved.

> Where animals are concerned we hold the view that the most highly developed have arisen from the lowest. . . . In the realm of mind, on the other hand, the primitive type is so commonly preserved alongside the transformations which have developed out of it that it is superfluous to give instances in proof of it. When this happens, it is usually the result of a bifurcation in development. One quantitative part of an attitude or an impulse has survived unchanged while another has undergone further development. This brings us very close to the more general problem of conservation in the mind. . . . Since the time when we recognized the error of supposing that ordinary forgetting signified destruction or annihilation of the memory-trace, we have been inclined to the opposite view that nothing once formed in the mind could ever perish, that everything survives in some way or other, and is capable under certain conditions of being brought to light again . . . (Freud, *Civilization and Its Discontents*, pp. 14–15).

What has now come to be common sense is that in everyman there is the potentiality for criminality, and that these are neither accidents nor visitations of degeneracy, but products of a delicate balance of forces that, under different circumstances, might have produced normality or even saintliness. Good and evil, in short, grow from a common root.

Freud's genius was in his resolution of polarities. The distinction of child and adult was one such. It did not suffice to reiterate that the child was father to the man. The theory of infantile sexuality and the stages of psychosexual development were an effort to fill the gap, the latter clumsy, the former elegant. Though the alleged progression of sexual expression from the oral, to the anal, to the phallic, and finally to the genital has not found a secure place either in common sense or in general psychology, the developmental continuity of sexuality has been recognised by both. Common sense honors the continuity in the baby-books and in the permissiveness with which young parents of today resolve their doubts. And the research of Beach and others has shown the profound effects of infantile experience on adult sexual behaviour – even in lower organisms.

If today people are reluctant to report their dreams with the innocence once attached to such recitals, it is again because Freud brought into common question the discontinuity between the rational purposefulness of waking life and the seemingly irrational purposelessness of fantasy and dream. While the crude symbolism of Freud's early efforts at dream interpretation has come increasingly to be abandoned – that telephone poles and tunnels have an invariant sexual reference – the conception of the dream as representing disguised wishes and fears has become common coin. And Freud's recognition of deep unconscious processes in the creative act, let it also be said, has gone far toward enriching our understanding of the kinship between the artist, the humanist, and the man of science.

Finally, it is our heritage from Freud that the all-or-none distinction between mental illness and mental health has been replaced by a more humane conception of the continuity of these states. The view that neurosis is a severe reaction to human trouble is as revolutionary in its implications for social practice as it is daring in formulation. The 'bad seed' theories, the nosologies of the nineteenth century, the demonologies and doctrines of divine punishment – none of these provided a basis for compassion toward human suffering comparable to that of our time.

One may argue, at last, that Freud's sense of the continuity of human conditions, of the likeness of the human plight, has made possible a deeper sense of the brotherhood of man. It has in any case tempered the spirit of punitiveness toward what once we took as evil

F.—6*

and what we now see as sick. We have not yet resolved the dilemma posed by these two ways of viewing. Its resolution is one of the great moral challenges of our age.

Why, after such initial resistance, were Freud's views so phenomenally successful in transforming common conceptions of man?

One reason we have already considered: the readiness of the Western world to accept a naturalistic explanation of organic phenomena and, concurrently, to be readier for such explanation in the mental sphere. There had been at least four centuries of uninterrupted scientific progress, recently capped by a theory of evolution that brought man into continuity with the rest of the animal kingdom. The rise of naturalism as a way of understanding nature and man witnessed a corresponding decline in the explanatory aspirations of religion. By the close of the nineteenth century, religion, to use Morton White's phrase, 'too often agreed to accept the role of a non-scientific spiritual grab-bag, or an ideological know-nothing'. The elucidation of the human plight had been abandoned by religion and not yet adopted by science.

It was the inspired imagery, the proto-theory of Freud that was to fill the gap. Its success in transforming the common conception of man was not simply its recourse to the 'cause-and-effect' discourse of science. Rather it is Freud's imagery, I think, that provides the clue to this ideological power. It is an imagery of necessity, one that combines the dramatic, the tragic, and the scientific views of necessity. It is here that Freud's intellectual heritage matters so deeply. Freud's is a theory or a proto-theory peopled with actors. The characters are from life: the blind, energic, pleasure-seeking id; the priggish and punitive super-ego; the ego, battling for its being by diverting the energy of the others to its own use. The drama has an economy and a terseness. The ego develops canny mechanisms for dealing with the threat of id impulses: denial, projection, and the rest. Balances are struck between the actors, and in the balance is character and neurosis. Freud was using the dramatic technique of decomposition, the play whose actors are parts of a single life. It is a technique that he himself had recognised in fantasies and dreams, one he honoured in 'The Poet and the Daydream'.

The imagery of the theory, moreover, has an immediate resonance with the dialectic of experience. True, it is not the stuff of superficial conscious experience. But it fits the human plight, its conflictedness, its private torment, its impulsiveness, its secret and frightening urges, its tragic quality.

Concerning its scientific imagery, it is marked by the necessity of the classical mechanics. At times the imagery is hydraulic: suppress this stream of impulses, and perforce it breaks out in a displacement elsewhere. The system is a closed and mechanical one. At times it is electrical, as when cathexes are formed and withdrawn like electrical charges. The way of thought fitted well the common-sense physics of its age.

Finally, the image of man presented was thoroughly secular; its ideal type was the mature man free of infantile neuroticism, capable of finding his own way. This freedom from both Utopianism and asceticism has earned Freud the contempt of ideological totalitarians of the Right and the Left. But the image has found a ready home in the rising, liberal intellectual middle class. For them, the Freudian ideal type has become a rallying point in the struggle against spiritual regimentation.

I have said virtually nothing about Freud's equation of sexuality and impulse. It was surely and still is a stimulus to resistance. But to say that Freud's success lay in forcing a reluctant Victorian world to accept the importance of sexuality is as empty as hailing Darwin for his victory over fundamentalism. Each had a far more profound effect.

Can Freud's contribution to the common understanding of man in the twentieth century be likened to the impact of such great physical and biological theories as Newtonian physics and Darwin's conception of evolution? The question is an empty one. Freud's mode of thought is not a theory in the conventional sense, it is a metaphor, an analogy, a way of conceiving man, a drama. I would propose that Anaximander is the proper parallel: his view of the connectedness of physical nature was also an analogy – and a powerful one. Freud is the ground from which theory will grow, and he has prepared the twentieth century to nurture the growth. But far more important, he has provided an image of man that has made him comprehensible without at the same time making him contemptible.

SOURCE: *Partisan Review* (Summer 1956).

THOMAS S. SZASZ

Freud as a Leader (1963)

I MUST ask you to set aside, in your mind, the contributions of psychoanalysis to science, and let your thoughts wander back along the path this discipline followed as it evolved. This exercise may result in some profitable insights about the sort of leadership which promoted the development of psychoanalysis, the sort of leadership now directing it, and perhaps, by inference, also about the sort of leadership it ought to have.

The initial basic discoveries of psychoanalysis were all made and published before 1906. In the course of little more than a decade – during the years which Freud called a period of 'splendid isolation' – there was placed before the scientific world, as well as the general public, the classic ideas on hysteria, repression and the unconscious, dream theory, and the so-called theory of infantile sexuality. Other impressions to the contrary notwithstanding, Freud encountered no difficulties in publishing any of these ideas. Furthermore, most of his writings were favorably received – though naturally they evoked much indignation, also – and soon they aroused the widespread interest they deserved. What happened next in psychoanalysis was, in my opinion, of fateful consequence.

What happened was that Freud abandoned the kind of leadership we associate with the progress of science and adopted in its stead the kind of leadership typical of big business or of imperialistic nationalism. How did this monopolistic-nationalistic leadership manifest itself? In order to answer this question, let us adopt the jargon of commercial enterprise and apply it to the psychoanalytic movement.

The first phase of psychoanalysis, the period prior to approximately 1906, may now be regarded as the period of *product development*. It is as if Freud had developed the formula for, say, Coca Cola (or sulfanilamide) and found that, within a narrow circle, there was

considerable interest in it and demand for it. He must have decided
that his next task was to *sell* his product to a wider range of customers
than could be reached with the relatively simple techniques of ad-
vertising that he had been using – that is, by merely publishing his
observations and ideas. A stock company, the International Psychoanalytic Association, was then formed, with the purpose of promoting
and distributing psychoanalysis.

Freud, of course, was the majority stockholder, with Ferenczi,
Adler, Jung, Abraham, and Stekel being the other principal stock-
holders. The first order of business was to give the firm a pleasing
public image. There were, as will be recalled, two reasons for this.
First, Freud and most of his early colleagues were Jews; second,
psychoanalysis had to do with sex. Neither Jewishness nor sexuality
was considered attractive in Central Europe in those days.

How did Freud proceed to create an attractive corporate image for
organised psychoanalysis? He did this by setting up a dummy corporation headed by a front-man chosen especially to inspire confidence
and respectability. This public relations manoeuvre was intended to
camouflage both the Jewishness and the socially subversive qualities
of the organisation.

Freud himself explained his motives for acting in this manner,
and they are not difficult to understand. Here was a Jewish firm,
psychoanalysis, that wanted to do business with anti-Semitic customers,
that is, the German-speaking medical world and their patients. Freud
was in a position much like that of an American firm of Jewish owner-
ship that wanted to do business in, say, Saudi Arabia. Obviously, in
such a circumstance the thing to do is set up a dummy corporation,
headed by a non-Jew, preferably even an anti-Semite. Thus was Carl
Gustav Jung selected to be the first president of the International
Psychoanalytic Association in 1910.

When Freud announced his plan to make Jung president, his Viennese
colleagues passionately disagreed. Perhaps the Viennese had a *scientific*
organisation in mind, headed by a person most expressive of the group's
scientific ideals. But Freud was organising a *movement*, and he frankly
said so. Before the issue came to a vote, the Viennese group held a
protest meeting to prevent Jung's election to the presidency. When
Freud heard of this, he rushed to Stekel's hotel room, where the group
congregated, and, according to Jones,

made an impassioned appeal for their adherence. He laid stress on the virulent hostility that surrounded them and the need for outside support to counter it. Then dramatically throwing back his coat he declared: 'My enemies would be willing to see me starve; they would tear my very coat off my back.'

Note Freud's appeal to economic rather than to scientific considerations. Jung was needed for business, not for scientific reasons.

I might interject here that there were no scientific reasons, at that time, for Freud's adopting such an expansionist policy. His work was becoming ever more widely known. Nor had he experienced any difficulties in publishing his views. His motives, I submit, were partly economic – his practice was not particularly good until after the First World War – and partly imperialistic – he wanted to spread psychoanalysis as a medical-moral-psychological movement as far and wide as possible.

But let us continue with the Jung affair. In order to see the sort of leadership Freud himself exercised with respect to his colleagues, it is necessary to examine his own version of the foregoing events. In his essay, 'On the History of the Psycho-Analytic Movement' (1914), Freud wrote:

> What I had in mind was to organize the psychoanalytic movement, to transfer its centre to Zurich and to give it a chief who would look after its future career. As this scheme has met with much opposition among the adherents of psychoanalysis, I will set out my reasons for it in some detail. I hope that these will justify me, even though it turns out that what I did was in fact not very wise.

He then described Jung's qualifications for the post – such as his proven contributions, his talent, his energy, and so forth. 'In addition to this,' added Freud, 'he seemed ready to enter into a friendly relationship with me and for my sake to give up certain racial prejudices which he had previously permitted himself.'

I find this amusing. I say this because I regard Freud too highly to believe that he could have had such a naïve view of religious or race prejudice. In the passage quoted, Freud referred to Jung's anti-Semitism as if it were an old piece of furniture that Jung had promised to discard. But the discoverer of the unconscious must have known better. If Jung was indeed somewhat anti-Semitic, this was not something he could promise to give up, just like that. It is worthwhile for us to ask, further, what sort of impression this manoeuvre must have made on Jung? For a Swiss-German to be used so crudely and un-ashamedly to promote an enterprise which its real owner regarded as essentially Jewish could have only served to corroborate Jung's anti-Semitic imagery of the 'scheming, unscrupulous Jew,' an image of which Hitler was to make such full use.

The International Psychoanalytic Association having been estab-lished, and branch societies having been formed, the widespread promotion of psychoanalysis seemed to be well launched. But no sooner was the venture incorporated than it ran into trouble. As official psychoanalytic history has it, the difficulty was that Adler and Jung developed ideas too radically different from those considered characteristic of psychoanalysis. Thus, in the interests of the 'purity' of psychoanalysis, a separation had to be made between genuine Freudian psychoanalysis and modifications of it.

This view presupposes, of course, certain distinctions between psychoanalysis proper and variations of it. Here our commercial model of product-development, promotion, distribution, and so forth, should prove very illuminating. For, as soon as the psycho-analytic business was launched, the distributors – that is, men like Adler, Jung, Stekel, and others – refused to abide by the original patent specifications. To Freud, psychoanalysis was like an invention, which the inventor could patent, thus restricting the rights of others in its use. Thus, Freud insisted that psychoanalysis was to be dispensed only in accordance with his specifications. But he went even further: he declared that only he, and no one else, could change or modify the original formula.

It is hardly surprising that most of Freud's colleagues, whom he appointed as his franchised distributors of psychoanalysis, had loftier aspirations. They were all intelligent and well trained men, and most of them were heretical characters to boot. No sooner had the distri-butors gotten hold of their merchandise, they started to tamper with it. Next, they announced that they had modified the original formula – we see this kind of thing nowadays in the development of new anti-biotics – and declared that their new product was better than the ori-ginal. In this way, one distributor after another went into research and development work, and then set up manufacturing facilities for his own particular brand of modified psychoanalysis.

If Freud had been satisfied to be a scientific investigator of human behavior, he would have had no cause for objection. Indeed, he ought to have rejoiced that his ideas proved so fertile, that they stimulated so much investigation in areas hitherto neglected by scientists. Domagk, the discoverer of the sulfonamids, ushered in a new era of chemotherapy As a result of the work he stimulated, the patent rights on sulfanilamide resulted only in limited revenues for the chemical firm that held them. Yet, no chemist or medical man would have dreamed of complaining that sulfanilamide, the original sulfone drug, was being ruined; nor would they have claimed that only Domagk had a right to change its formula!

In so far as certain kinds of scientific discoveries and technological inventions can be patented, this only means that, as sources of revenue, the discoveries or inventions shall primarily bring reward to those who discovered or developed them. As contributions to human knowledge, the fruits of science and technology cannot be patented. In other words, the essentially non-commercial uses to which science and technology may be put – for example, in teaching new knowledge or new skills to others – cannot be restricted by patents. For this reason, scientific theories and psychotherapeutic techniques – the only two commodities to which Freud could lay claim as an inventor – cannot be patented. This simple fact must have caused Freud much pain. For he adopted a highly monopolistic attitude toward psychoanalysis and tried to restrict its use to those whom he considered loyal disciples. In other words ,in effect Freud tried to patent psychoanalysis. Naturally, he failed. Unfortunately, however, he did succeed in setting an example, so that many of his followers have also tried to patent their ideas. This resulted in a basically faulty development in psychiatry as a social science, and the founding of numerous schools of psychoanalysis – instead of each worker more modestly contributing his little building blocks to the house of science.

Freud's attempt to patent psychoanalysis may be illustrated by his controversy with Adler. The same controversy was later repeated over and over again, with Jung, with Stekel, with Rank, and finally with Ferenczi, the 'Crown Prince', himself. Meanwhile, Abraham died, Sachs was passive, so really Jones alone, among the originally franchised distributors, proved to be reliable. Then, during the post-Freudian era, the same controversy over patent-rights continued between the original patent-holders (the American Psychoanalytic Association) and Horney, Sullivan, Fromm, and others.

Exactly why did Freud object to Adler? The facts simply are that Adler had somewhat different ideas about psychology and psychotherapy than Freud. This, of course, does not explain anything. Freud and Adler could still have proceeded with their work, as other scientists do. Oppenheimer and Teller differed on the feasibility of the hydrogen bomb, but this did not mean that either man's stature as a physicist suffered, or that they could no longer both belong to the same scientific organisation.

If we look at these events sort of naïvely, they are quite puzzling. Why did these people fight with each other all the time? The best answer seems to be that they fought over fame and money. Freud was really very much like the early American business tycoons. Here is his explanation, in his own words, of his objection to Adler: 'I wish merely to show that these theories controvert the fundamental principles of analysis (and on what points they controvert them) and that for this reason they should not be known by the name of analysis.'

So the issue was not whether Adler was right or wrong, but what should be *called* psychoanalysis. It was as if Freud had patented Coca Cola. He did not really care whether Pepsi Cola or Royal Cola or Crown Cola were better. He merely wanted to make sure that only his products carried the *original label*.

I do not think I exaggerate. Consider the following passage, in which Freud contrasts the differences between Freudian and Adlerian psychoanalysis:

> The first task confronting psychoanalysis was to explain the neuroses; it used the two facts of resistance and transference as starting-points, and taking into consideration the third fact of amnesia, accounted for them with its theories of repression, of the sexual motive forces in neurosis and of the unconscious. Psychoanalysis has never claimed to provide a complete theory of human mentality in general, but only expected that what it offered should be applied to supplement and correct the knowledge acquired by other means. Adler's theory, however, goes far beyond this point, it seeks at one stroke to explain the behaviour and character of human beings as well as their neurotic and psychotic illness.

This is a pretty fantastic argument. Here is Freud, in 1914, criticizing Adler for failing to confine himself to explanations of the neuroses, and for offering a general theory of human behavior. But of course Freud did not limit himself to the neuroses either, and he too tried to develop a general theory of human behavior. Ten years before his criticism of Adler's work, Freud published *The Psychopathology of Everyday Life* (1904); in 1911 the Schreber case; in 1912–13, *Totem and Taboo*; and in 1914 a short paper on 'The Moses of Michelangelo'. Are these contributions to our understanding of neurosis or to our understanding of human behavior generally?

How was this patent-infringement suit against Adler decided? It could not be settled legally, since scientific theories of human behavior are not patentable. It so happened, moreover, that at the time of the Freud–Adler conflict, which occurred in 1911, Freud held no official position in psychoanalysis. In a truly Machiavellian spirit, he preferred to operate behind the scenes. The president of the International Psychoanalytic Association was Jung, and the president of the Vienna Psychoanalytic Society was Adler. But these men were, as I suggested, merely the franchised dealers and representatives of the powerful owner and behind-the-scenes board chairman of the corporation. If the dealers misbehaved, Freud could withdraw their franchises. This is exactly what he did. As a member – though admittedly a very special sort of member – of the Vienna Psychoanalytic Society, Freud found himself in serious disagreement with Adler, the president of the society. Now Freud had several choices. He could have waited until Adler's term expired, and then could have brought pressure on the membership to prevent his re-election. Or he could have himself resigned. If he had taken Adler's presidency seriously, he would have been honour bound to take one or the other of these steps. But Freud preferred an open showdown, for he wanted to discredit Adler as a representative of psychoanalysis. Only in this light – that is, as a symbolic act of discrediting – does Freud's forcing of Adler's resignation make sense.

In spite of these facts, Jones chose to interpret Freud's attitudes about leadership as follows:

Freud greatly disliked occupying any prominent position, especially if it might bring with it any duties that implied the ruling of other people. – But as the founder of his new methods and theories, and with his wealth of experience and knowledge behind him, his position in the little circle of Viennese followers could not fail to be an exceptionally dominating one.

Although Freud's tendency to autocratic leadership has often been commented on – it has been ably discussed, for example, by Fromm – it seems to me that insufficient light has been cast on the way in which Freud exercised leadership. It was not so much that he was autocratic or tyrannical. Overt tyranny can be appraised for what it is, and there are many ways of resisting it. Freud's leadership, however, was deceitful. He created a pseudo-democratic, pseudo-scientific atmosphere, but was careful to retain for himself the power to decide all important issues. The disguised nature of Freud's political leadership is what gave rise to so much confusion and misunderstanding.

It seems to me that Freud managed the affairs of the psychoanalytic movement as a Caribbean dictator, called upon to democratise his regime, might conduct his government. Such a dictator might appoint a president and a cabinet; he might even appoint a person to be the leader of an opposition party. The result would be a mock parliamentary system, with the dictator, retaining all the real power, now operating from behind the scenes rather than openly. Once more, if this seems exaggerated, consider Freud's own account of how Jung became president, which I quoted earlier: 'What I had in mind was to organize the psychoanalytic movement, to transfer its centre to Zurich and to *give it* a chief who would look after its future career.' (Emphasis supplied.)

But how can one person appoint another as *chief*, unless he is himself the chief? And what sort of chief is he who, should he displease one particular member of the group, can be dismissed by that member? Freud's essential concept of leadership seemed to be to bestow tokens of power on his competitors, only to discredit them if they dared to use it. About Adler he wrote:

> As an instance of the 'persecution' to which he asserts he has been subjected by me, I can point out the fact that after the Association was founded *I made over to him the leadership of the Vienna group*. It was not until urgent demands were put forward by all the members of the society that *I let myself be persuaded* to take the chair again at its scientific meetings. (Emphasis supplied.)

This tendency to secret oligarchic control, with figurehead appointed leaders, has characterized all of the subsequent history of organizational psychoanalysis.

I cannot trace here, in all its ramifications, the relevance of the model

of an international cartel to the psychoanalytic organisation which
Freud founded and which is still with us today. I should like, however,
to run through, in summary fashion, the various phases of psychoanalytic history, as seen from this point of view.

1. I have already commented on the first period, ending with the
First World War, during which Freud, the man in control of the cartel,
objected to several of his distributors on the grounds that they sold
goods that were illegitimately manufactured and improperly labeled.
At this time, psychoanalysts were protecting their market from, as it
were, Japanese imports.

2. As a result of this process, the franchises of several distributors
were withdrawn. Thus, Jung and Adler, and later Horney, Sullivan,
and Fromm were refused recognition as franchised dealers in psychoanalysis.

3. After the Second World War a new type of conflict developed
between the cartel and some of its distributors. Since few analysts
really cared any more about what was psychoanalysis and what was
something else – the cartel having, as it were, absorbed most of its
competitors – product labeling was no longer a problem. Instead, the
conflict now centered on the identity of the customers to whom the
product was distributed, fearing that some might redistribute it and
thus become psychoanalysts without having been properly franchised
by the cartel. I refer, of course, to the problem of psychoanalytic
practice by non-medical analysts. Although the official policy in the
United States had always been to train only physicians in psychoanalysis,
there was considerable 'bootleg' training of non-medical personnel.
In the early 1950s the American Psychoanalytic Association threatened
those engaged in such so-called unauthorised training with the loss of
their franchise – that is, with expulsion from the Association. The
power of the Association to translate this threat into action was called
into question, and was eventually frustrated – largely through the
efforts of Clara Thompson.

It is significant to note, in this connection, that in 1911, when the
psychoanalytic cartel was weak, it was only too glad to sell to anyone,
and especially to psychologists, whereas in the 1950s secure in its power
and self-sterilised of scientific controversy, the cartel exercised its
authority by attempting to regulate not only what was psychoanalysis
and who could sell it, but even *to whom* it could be sold. Thus it was

decreed that psychoanalysis ought not be distributed to certain custo-mers. This discrimination, especially against psychologists, is truly ironic, considering that the standard edition of Freud's works is called 'The Complete *Psychological* Works of Sigmund Freud'. In sum, then, the prohibition against teaching psychoanalysis to non-medical persons is the ultimate symbolisation of the psychoanalytic organisa-tion's commercialistic rather than scientific leadership.

Has all this other than historical interest for us today? I believe it has. In the first place, we ought no longer to shirk our responsibility to recognise tyranny and false leadership in the organisational history and tradition of psychoanalysis. Einstein aptly observed that 'the only rational way of educating is to be an example – of what to avoid, if one can't be the other sort.'

In scientific leadership Freud gave us an example of what to avoid. In 'The History of the Psycho-Analytic Movement' (1914), he wrote: 'Adler's 'Individual Psychology' is now one of the many schools of psychology which are adverse to psychoanalysis and its fuller develop-ment is of no concern of ours.' Is this the proper posture of a scientific leader? Persons who advocate this sort of discrediting of the investiga-tions of their colleagues sever their loyalty to science and condemn themselves as propagandists whose example should be a warning, not an ideal, to students. In a similar vein, Freud wrote to Ferenczi, in 1913: 'We possess the truth; I am as sure of it as fifteen years ago.'

We all have a pretty good idea of the freedom-loving, experimental non-dogmatic, democratic sort of model that liberatarians in all walks of life have described for us, first in Greek antiquity, and with renewed vigor since the Enlightenment. Instead of rephrasing this model in my own words, I should like to quote for you a beautiful statement of it by Professor Richard Feynman. In an essay entitled 'The Value of Science' (1956) he wrote:

> We are at the very beginning of time for the human race. It is not un-reasonable that we grapple with problems. There are tens of thousands of years in the future. . . . *It is our responsibility to leave the men of the future a free hand. In the impetuous youth of humanity we can make grave errors that can stunt our growth for a long time. This we will do if we say we have the answers now* . . . and thus doom man for a long time to the chains of authority, confined to the limits of our present imagination. . . . It is our responsibility

as scientists, knowing the great progress and great value of a satisfactory philosophy of ignorance, the great progress that is the fruit of freedom of thought, to proclaim the value of this freedom, to teach how doubt is not to be feared but welcomed and discussed and to demand this freedom as our duty to all coming generations. (Emphasis supplied.)

I submit, therefore, that psychoanalysts ought to protest against the efforts of those who would make of this discipline something special and sacred. The contributions of psychoanalysis to the science of human behavior are, of course, substantial. But nevertheless – or perhaps precisely because of it – the proposition that psychoanalysis is a discrete and separate science must be considered an absurdity. Freud, the Freudians, and the post-Freudians have all contributed to the science of man. But let us recognise that insofar as they have also shown a special loyalty to psychoanalysis itself – as something other than a part of the study of man – they betrayed their faith in science and in humanity. Such loyalty can be purchased only at the cost of disloyalty to the ideals of the open society.

Freud always spoke of psychoanalysis as his personal discovery, as though it were a vein of gold that he was the first to stake out. His last work, *An Outline of Psychoanalysis* (1939), which he left unfinished at his death, is a heroic attempt to re-establish his claim to the property he first staked out more than a half-century before. Freud thus exemplified the posture of the entrepreneur or of the empire-builder, not of the scientist.

The scientist can only rejoice if his discoveries and ideas diffuse into the world at large and become the common property of mankind. But they shall then no longer belong to him nor to any group founded by him.

Georg Simmel, a sociologist and contemporary of Freud's, expressed this credo well when he wrote in his diary:

I know that I will die without intellectual heirs – and that is as it should be. My legacy will be as it were in cash, distributed to many heirs, each transforming his part into use conforming to his own nature: a use that will no longer reveal its indebtedness to this heritage.

SOURCE: *Antioch Review*, XXIII, No. 2 (Summer 1963).

W. H. AUDEN

In Memory of Sigmund Freud

(d. Sept. 1939)

When there are so many we shall have to mourn,
when grief has been made so public, and exposed
    to the critique of a whole epoch
      the frailty of our conscience and anguish,

of whom shall we speak? For every day they die
among us, those who were doing us some good,
    who knew it was never enough but
      hoped to improve a little by living.

Such was this doctor, still at eighty he wished
to think of our life from whose unruliness
    so many plausible young futures
      with threats or flattery ask obedience,

but his wish was denied him: he closed his eyes
upon that last picture, common to us all,
    of problems like relatives gathered
      puzzled and jealous about our dying.

For about him till the very end were still
those he had studied, the fauna of the night,
    and shades that still waited to enter
      the bright circle of his recognition

turned elsewhere with their disappointment as he
was taken away from his life interest
    to go back to the earth in London,
      an important Jew who died in exile.

Only Hate was happy, hoping to augment
his practice now, and his dingy clientele
    who think they can be cured by killing
  and covering the gardens with ashes.

They are still alive, but in a world he changed
simply by looking back with no false regrets;
    all he did was to remember
  like the old and be honest like children.

He wasn't clever at all: he merely told
the unhappy Present to recite the Past
    like a poetry lesson till sooner
  or later it faltered at the line where

long ago the accusations had begun,
and suddenly knew by whom it had been judged,
    how rich life had been and how silly,
  and was life-forgiven and more humble,

able to approach the Future as a friend
without a wardrobe of excuses, without
    a set mask of rectitude or an
  embarrassing over-familiar gesture.

No wonder the ancient cultures of conceit
in his technique of unsettlement foresaw
    the fall of princes, the collapse of
  their lucrative patterns of frustration:

if he succeeded, why, the Generalised Life
would become impossible, the monolith
    of State be broken and prevented
  the co-operation of avengers.

Of course they called on God, but he went his way
down among the lost people like Dante, down
    to the stinking fosse where the injured
  lead the ugly life of the rejected,

and showed us what evil is, not, as we thought,
deeds that must be punished, but our lack of faith,
     our dishonest mood of denial,
   the concupiscence of the oppressor.

If some traces of the autocratic pose,
the paternal strictness he distrusted, still
     clung to his utterance and features,
   it was a protective coloration

for one who'd lived among enemies so long:
if often he was wrong and, at times, absurd,
     to us he is no more a person
   now but a whole climate of opinion

under whom we conduct our different lives:
Like weather he can only hinder or help,
     the proud can still be proud but find it
   a little harder, the tyrant tries to

make do with him but doesn't care for him much:
he quietly surrounds all our habits of growth
     and extends, till the tired in even
   the remotest miserable duchy

have felt the change in their bones and are cheered,
till the child, unlucky in his little State,
     some hearth where freedom is excluded,
   a hive whose honey is fear and worry,

feels calmer now and somehow assured of escape,
while, as they lie in the grass of our neglect,
     so many long-forgotten objects
   revealed by his undiscouraged shining

are returned to us and made precious again;
games we had thought we must drop as we grew up,
     little noises we dared not laugh at,
   faces we made when no one was looking.

But he wishes us more than this. To be free
is often to be lonely. He would unite
        the unequal moieties fractured
    by our own well-meaning sense of justice,

would restore to the larger the wit and will
the smaller possesses but can only use
        for arid disputes, would give back to
    the son the mother's richness of feeling:

but he would have us remember most of all
to be enthusiastic over the night,
        not only for the sense of wonder
    it alone has to offer, but also

because it needs our love. With large sad eyes
its delectable creatures look up and beg
        us dumbly to ask them to follow:
    they are exiles who long for the future

that lies in our power, they too would rejoice
if allowed to serve enlightenment like him,
        even to bear our cry of 'Judas',
    as he did and all must bear who serve it.

One rational voice is dumb. Over his grave
the household of Impulse mourns one dearly loved:
        sad is Eros, builder of cities,
    and weeping anarchic Aphrodite.

SOURCE: W. H. Auden, *Collected Shorter Poems 1927–1957* (1967).

Select Bibliography

Ola Andersson, *Studies in the Prehistory of Psychoanalysis: The Aetiology of the Psychoneuroses and Some Related Themes in Sigmund Freud's Scientific Writings and Letters, 1886–1896* (Svenska Bokfor Laget, Stockholm, 1962).

Percival Bailey, *Sigmund, The Unserene* (Charles C. Thomas, 1965).

David Bakan, *Sigmund Freud and the Jewish Mystical Tradition* (Van Nostrand, 1958).

Ludwig Binswanger, *Sigmund Freud: Reminiscences of a Friendship* (Grune & Stratton, 1957).

John C. Burnham, *Psychoanalysis in American Medicine 1894–1918: Medicine, Science and Culture* (International Universities Press, 1967).

Roland Dalbiez, *Psychoanalytic Method and the Doctrine of Freud* (Longmans Green, 1941).

Henri Ellenberger, *The Discovery of the Unconscious* (Basic Books, 1970; Allen Lane, 1971).

The Freud Journal of Lou Andreas-Salome (Basic Books, 1964).

Eric Fromm, *Sigmund Freud's Mission: An Analysis of His Personality and Influence* (Harper, 1959).

Muriel Gardiner (ed.), *The Wolf Man and Sigmund Freud* (Hogarth Press, 1972).

A. Grinstein, *On Freud's Dreams* (Wayne University Press, 1968).

H. D. *Tribute to Freud* (Pantheon Books, 1956; Carcenet Press, 1971).

Mary Higgins and Chester M. Raphael (eds.), *Reich Speaks of Freud* (Noonday Press, 1967).

Frederick J. Hoffman, *Freudianism and the Literary Imagination* (Louisiana University Press, 1957).

Stanley Edgar Hyman, *The Tangled Bank* (Athenaeum, 1962).

Ernest Jones, *Free Associations* (Hogarth Press, 1959).

Ernest Jones, *The Life and Work of Sigmund Freud*, 3 vols. (Hogarth Press, 1958).

Peter Madison, *Freud's Concept of Repression and Defence* (University of Minnesota Press, 1961).

Clauda C. Morrison, *Freud and the Critic* (University of North Carolina Press, 1969).

162   SELECT BIBLIOGRAPHY

Benjamin Nelson (ed.), *Freud and the Twentieth Century* (Allen & Unwin, 1958).
C. P. Oberndorf, *A History of Psychoanalysis in America* (Grune & Stratton, 1953).
Philip Rieff, *Freud: The Mind of the Moralist* (Viking, 1959).
David Riesman, *Individualism Reconsidered* (The Free Press, 1954).
Paul Roazen, *Freud: Political and Social Thought* (Vintage Books, 1968).
Hans Sachs, *Freud, Master and Friend* (Harvard University Press, 1944).
D. Shakow and D. Rapaport, *The Influence of Freud on American Psychology* (International Universities Press, 1964; Meridian Books, 1964).
Walter A. Stewart, *Psychoanalysis: The First Ten Years, 1888-1898* (Allen & Unwin, 1969).
Lionel Trilling, *Freud and the Crisis of Our Culture* (Beacon Press, 1955).
Lancelot Law Whyte, *The Unconscious Before Freud* (Tavistock Publications, 1962).
Richard Wollheim, *Freud* (Fontana/Collins, 1971).
Joseph Wortis, *Fragments of an Analysis with Freud* (Simon & Schuster, 1954).

LETTERS

Freud's own letters are to be found in the following books.
A Psychoanalytic Dialogue: the Letters of Sigmund Freud and Karl Abraham (Hogarth Press, 1965).
The Origins of Psychoanalysis: Letters, Notes and Drafts to Wilhelm Fliess (Hogarth Press, 1965). This volume contains the 'Project for a Scientific Psychology'.
Psychoanalysis and Faith: The Letters of Sigmund Freud and Oskar Pfister (Hogarth Press, 1963).
The Letters of Sigmund Freud and Arnold Zweig (Hogarth Press, 1970).
Letters of Sigmund Freud 1873-1939 (Hogarth Press, 1965).

Notes on Contributors

JEROME S. BRUNER, Professor of Psychology, Harvard University; publications include: *Opinions and Personality, A Study of Thinking, Mandate from the People, The Relevance of Learning.*

IAGO GALDSTON, M.D., Chief of Psychiatric Training, Department of Mental Health, State of Connecticut; editor of *Psychoanalysis in Present Day Psychology.*

IDA MACALPINE, formerly psychiatrist at St Bartholomew's Hospital, London; author (with Richard Hunter) of *Schizophrenia 1677, Three Hundred Years of British Psychiatry, George III and the Mad Business.*

JACQUES RIVIÈRE (1866–1925), began his association with the *Nouvelle Revue Française* in 1911; became editor in 1919.

GEORGE SANTAYANA (1863–1952), author of *The Life of Reason, Winds of Doctrine, Character and Opinion in the United States, Realms of Being.*

THOMAS S. SZASZ, Professor of Psychiatry at the State University of New York, Upstate Medical Centre, in Syracuse and a practising therapist; author of *Pain and Pleasure: A Study of Bodily Feelings, The Myth of Mental Illness, The Manufacture of Madness.*

LIONEL TRILLING, Professor of English at Columbia University; author of *Matthew Arnold, The Liberal Imagination, Beyond Culture, Sincerity and Authenticity.*

JOHN WISDOM, Professor of Philosophy, University of Oregon, formerly Professor of Philosophy, University of Cambridge; author of *Other Minds, Philosophy and Psycho-Analysis, Paradox and Discovery.*

Index